SET FREE TO
THRIVE

Your story matters!
Thrive in Christ!
Kaye

SET FREE TO THRIVE

EXCEEDING LIFE BEYOND
THIS WORLD OF CHAOS

KAYE M. CARTER

AUTHOR
ACADEMY elite

Printed in the United States of America

Published by Author Academy Elite
PO Box 43, Powell, OH 43035
AuthorAcademyElite.com

ISBN 978-1-943526-69-7 Paperback
ISBN 978-1-943526-68-0 Hardback

Library of Congress Control Number 2016949080

Unless otherwise indicated, all Scripture quotations are taken from *The Holy Bible*, King James Version, adaptations by the author in brackets.

Scripture quotations marked (NIV) are taken from the Holy Bible, New International Version®, NIV®. Copyright © 1973, 1978, 1984, 2011 by Biblica, Inc.™ Used by permission of Zondervan. All rights reserved worldwide. www.zondervan.com. The "NIV" and "New International Version" are trademarks registered in the United States Patent and Trademark Office by Biblica, Inc.™

Scripture quotations marked (ESV) are from the ESV˙ Bible (*The Holy Bible*, English Standard Version˙), copyright © 2001 by Crossway, a publishing ministry of Good News Publishers. Used by permission. All rights reserved.

Scripture quotations marked (NLT) are taken from *The Holy Bible*, New Living Translation, copyright ©1996, 2004, 2007, 2013, 2015 by Tyndale House Foundation. Used by permission of Tyndale House Publishers, Inc., Carol Stream, Illinois 60188. All rights reserved.

Scripture quotations marked (NKJV) are taken from *The Holy Bible*, New King James Version®. Copyright © 1982 by Thomas Nelson. Used by permission. All rights reserved.

For my beloved husband, Gregory.
Christ loving me through you is a gift like none other.
He restores my soul.

Clarity is deviance.
Confusion is the norm.

CONTENTS

PART THREE—DISCOVER LIFE THAT THRIVES

FOREWORD

Since first meeting Kaye, I have come to appreciate this kindred soul. She is a deep thinker and woman of faith who speaks with substance. When I heard she wanted to write her story I knew it would be the type of book to impact the heart of readers from diverse backgrounds. Writing with candor and conviction, her love for God and others is clear; her passion for the souls of hurting people is palpable.

Set Free to Thrive is a book you will read and ponder—the kind that provides clear solutions to the soul's deepest questions. Kaye shares her journey of the broken way—the common path of disappointment, heartache and loss that leads to new life, enlightenment and joy. A passage made possible only when we're submitted to the power of God.

Her personal insight, understanding of people, and love for truth of the Scriptures combine to provide you a powerful framework for a new mindset. When applied, it will lead to your own life of vitality and freedom. With each chapter, you will be challenged to exceed what may have become your normal. You will learn to defy the chaos that seeks to destroy who you are and why you are here.

Prepare yourself for inner healing and life outside the confines of ordinary faith.

Prepare for a heart set free to thrive.

Kary Oberbrunner
Author of *The Elixir Project, Day Job to Dream Job, The Deeper Path,* and *Your Secret Name*

ACKNOWLEDGMENTS

Writing a book, like living life is not an individual venture. The complexity of the narrative can never be be foretold or foreseen, and un-packaging the story is a process facilitated by a lifetime of interactions. This book has been shaped by the contribution of countless people, but I would be remiss not to mention these.

To Jesus, my Savior—thank you for new life, and for trading your beauty for my ashes.

To Greg—thank you for believing in me and loving me like no one else.

To Rebecca, Brandon, Bailey and Allison—thank you for teaching me to let go and let God.

To Mom and Dad—thank you for being supportive throughout the saga.

To Emma, Addison, Avery, Elayne, and Lydia—thank you for sweetening the adventure.

To Kary, my coach, thank you for blazing the trail and for pushing me to be my best. To the brothers and sisters of the Igniting Souls tribe, thank you for the authenticity and camaraderie of the shared journey. To the ladies of *Cutting Through the Chaos* study groups, thank you for sharing your stories as they intersect with mine. To Roy, Sarah, Cindy, and Lori, Greg, and Mom thank you for your honesty and eye for detail in the editing process.

And to you, the reader, thank you for opening your heart and mind to the reality of God's transformational power. Keep pressing into Jesus for the freedom to thrive as the person you were created to be.

Now unto Him who is able to do exceeding abundantly
above all that we ask or think, according to the
power that works within us,
Unto Him be glory...

Ephesians 3:20-21

Note to the Reader

Life in captivity.

It's a concept most people would assert they've never experienced. After all, the vast majority of the world's population has never been incarcerated for criminal wrong doing or physically imprisoned against their will. But it's an important subject for each of us to explore. In fact, at the risk of sounding a bit melodramatic, I will assert that the quality of your life in time and for eternity depends on your willingness to explore your own captivity.

A crucial link exists between a life of vitality and a personal desire. The hunger for real insight into the true state of your whole heart and mind leads to authentic vision. Without this level of clarity, complete liberty is nothing more than wishful thinking; we will remain imprisoned by emotional and spiritual chains of confusion.

But how can we know we are trapped? These inner shackles parade as the immutable status quo—the way it's always been…the unhealthy thought patterns that have always been part of us….the dysfunctional relationships…the place of resignation to pain, failure and loss of hope. Even for people of faith, these are the clanging echoes of the clinging chains we drag through life. And they prevent our complete healing and freedom.

I know this because despite being a Christian, I spent far too many years unable to live in the fullness of who I was created to be. I wanted to thrive, but felt like I did well just to survive the chaos. Desperately needing someone to come along side of me and help me gain clarity, I did the best with what I knew. Mental and emotional bondage persisted despite all of my sincere Christian activity. I prayed, repented and forgave. I served others and gave. I studied and tried harder. And by the grace of God's divine strength, I persevered multiple trials and heartache.

But the fog persisted. I cried privately, smiled publicly and felt so alone in each storm.

My desire to "just understand" was perpetually thwarted. Pat answers seemed oversimplified and self-serving. If the Scriptures were true, which I wholeheartedly believed, then old things had passed away and I had become new through my faith in Jesus Christ.

Yet old thought patterns persisted and relational turmoil continued to war against my soul. I was falling apart on the inside, but had to pretend I was fine on the outside. The freedom and unconditional love necessary to discover and experience the abundance Jesus promised His followers was inhibited. The faith-based culture I'd experienced gave lip-service to authenticity. Nice people wearing their own masks had many packaged answers, but no strategic solutions to the core questions of my soul. And so I cried out to God. I begged Him for understanding that went beyond human intellect and anemic Christianity. I pled for my life to have meaning. I was tired of going through the motions.

And now I'm praying for you. I'm begging God to use these lessons learned in the trenches to encourage and equip you. I am praying that you will be set free from any of your own inner captivity. I desire for you, what He has given to me: Healing. Real vision. A life that thrives as I become the person I was created and called to be.

This book explores ten important questions that lead us to a place of introspection. In the process, I share ten keys that have unlocked the shackles of my own heart and the hearts of those with whom I've been privileged to minister God's healing power.

We all want to do more in life than just survive. Our deeper desire to thrive is inextricably linked to becoming all we were designed to be. Consequently, you must realize the process of discovery we are about to embark upon is a threat to the status quo on a number of levels. In the coming pages tactics of resistance will attempt to stop you from working with God as He opens the eyes of your heart. They will distract you and may deject you—but remember they cannot defeat you without your consent.

The choice is yours.

If you aren't a follower of Christ, I hope to help you become one. If you are a Christian, I hope to assist your growth as a child of God. Jesus came to rescue us, not only from the penalty of sin, but also from its confining power day-to-day. We can be spiritually transformed in a moment. But our mind, will, and emotions are seldom changed to the same extent of our spirits at the time we begin following Christ. This practical transformation in our lives is a process.

The good news is that you don't have to accept the effects of old wounds, the deceit of sin, and pervasive thoughts and habits. You don't have to succumb to the captivity of shame and pretense. Your relationships don't have to be based in unhealthy fear-based insecurity. You've been given the option to live in freedom and abundance because of the victory Jesus won for you.

Now open your heart and embrace it.

Exceed beyond normal life.

Let's thrive.

PART ONE

DEFEAT YOUR STATUS QUO

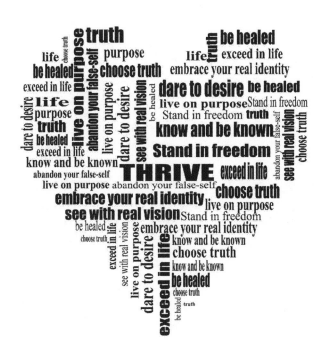

1

ONCE UPON A TIME
AND NOW

Are You Confused About Your Life Story?

*If I told you my story you would hear Hope that wouldn't let go.
And if I told you my story you would hear Love that never gave up.*

Big Daddy Weave, *My Story*, 2015

I was so confused. The story had taken a turn for which I had never planned. My mind was spiraling into the abyss of internal chaos. Tight bands of anguish restricted my breathing as I sat staring out the window. Once this had been my dream home nestled in the countryside, a haven of beauty and love. But frigid winds of change were howling again as I struggled to catch my breath.

The scene unfolding before my eyes seemed surreal and I felt as weathered as the old oak trees beyond the glass panes. The years of hot to cold cycles had culminated this time in a storm like none other. Silently and alone, I observed him stride toward the truck he'd rented to carry away his share of the stuff; the souvenirs of almost thirty years of life together. A low rumble of the engine jolted my frayed emotions and I watched the vehicle crawl down the winding driveway until it and our relationship faded from sight.

And then it was over.

The end.

No grand proclamation, "And they lived happily ever after."

So Long to the Fairy Tale

"Be still and know that I am God"...I heard it from deep within. None of this confusion was a shock to God. He knew, a new leg in the journey of my life was beginning—even if it did include circumstances for which I'd never planned. Despite the chaos seeking to suffocate me—I breathed deeply...my soul was inspired by the truth of God's Word. It infused life in that desperate hour and would sustain me yet again.

While my world had completely fallen apart, His plan continued to fall into place. Standing under the cold gray winter sky, I unwittingly took my first step on a path unlike any I'd ever traversed. The broken ending to the fairytale I'd been holding on to for so long had crushed my heart. With all energy to resist completely gone, God was positioning me to witness His glory. He was looking for a broken vessel out of which to shine.

And broken, I was.

After committing myself to God as a child, I'd lived my faith seriously. God and I had some history together; His unwavering faithfulness to me had been proven before. It had been the bedrock of my soul during years of circumstances threatening to consume my sanity, steal my joy and defeat my purpose. It was His love that motivated me during the toughest times, enabling me to thrive despite harsh disappointments and devastating betrayals of trust. Consequently, in the midst of that final storm of marital rejection I knew He was holding me close yet again.

So as the last vestiges of my illusion about the "happily ever after" were stripped away, I knew I had choices to be made. Just as every other person who ends up on an unchosen road, I had to choose a mindset. Would I choose to be a victim or victor? I could opt for bitterness and resentment, the frequent norm for the discarded middle-aged divorcée. Blame, entitlement and denial could become my favorite cards to play—or I could opt for something different. Would I allow my past to control my future by clinging to an illusion of "what might have been?" Or would I open a broken, yet grateful heart to the truth of an unknown story being written into my life by a God who loves me?

This is a defining choice we all are given in countless ways and in innumerable moments over the course of our lives. Far too often we choose bondage to the past because we refuse to open our fist and let go of the story *we* wanted to write within the scope of our own limited vision.

My choice was obvious, although not simple in that dark moment. I would overcome the blows of life by trusting in the truth of God's Word and in all the enlightenment it brings. But I've found that enlightenment can be a very difficult thing to embrace because it is greater vision for all things pertaining to this life and the world beyond.

> Far too often we choose bondage to the past because we refuse to open our fist and let go of the story *we* wanted to write within the scope of our own limited vision.

True enlightenment eradicates our ability to play mind games with ourselves in the misdirected attempt to shelter our lives from change or from unwanted facts. It demands removal of the rose-colored glasses with which we like to view ourselves. Enlightenment requires looking into the deepest recesses of our hearts and a willingness to deal with things we may have accepted as being part of us. And since it's a process that includes a lot of hard work, it often doesn't happen.

But when real crisis leads us to a place of complete desperation and dependence, we become thirsty. We are more likely to look up when flat on our back, broken from the illusion that everything was to end happily within the course of this life. And if we allow it, this can become the starting point to new vision and healing. I knew I needed God's insight if all of my broken pieces were ever to become connected again.

But the status quo vision of average Christianity was not going to do it for me this time; it certainly hadn't provided complete healing in the past. I knew many nice church people whose vision for the obscure was blinded by that which appears obvious. It produced an oversimplified, myopic view and a shallow culture that accepted a certain amount of captivity as normal.

In my darkest hour I was ready for a deeper look. I knew there had to be more than enduring publicly with a smile, while fighting back years of dammed-up tears threatening at any given moment to blow my cover. I desired truth and I wanted all of it—even if it did destroy the illusion of my own expectations to reveal my personal desperation and the limited scope of my vision.

Awakening Greater Expectations

Now what about you? Have you ever thought there might be more to life than meets the eye? As a Christian, have you ever felt slightly dissatisfied with the way the story of your life seems to be turning out? Perhaps it's never occurred to you, but each of our life stories is a one-and-only. You have been intrinsically wired with a purpose unique to you. And until you discover how to fulfill that purpose, you will continue to feel a longing for more.

We each are living a once-upon-a-time tale that matters for time and eternity. Yet many people give up and stop expecting much of anything. After a painful childhood or an unexpected blow from life, the deceit sets in. The thirst for more is satiated by lesser things. But now is the time to awaken and fully explore the truth of all that was intended for us, even if it will mean a change to our perceptions, and perhaps an altered comfort level with our status quo.

The beginning of my own personal epiphany came during dark seasons when I was filled with many questions of "why?" For years I had experienced life to be full of what seemed to be many inconsistencies between what I thought I knew about faith and my own reality. Long before my illusion-based dream was destroyed, God had opened my eyes to a foundational flaw within the Christian culture intertwined in my story.

While growing up in church, I'd been taught a simple, although perhaps inadvertently self-exalting, equation to "success." Success had been interpreted by me as a person's tale ending in the "happily ever after." This was otherwise known as God's blessing as defined by the North American Christian norm. Confusion in my mind had grown because, despite practicing the equation to the best degree

I knew possible, the fairy-tale failed to unfold according to expectation.

Have you ever been exposed to the same or a similar oversimplified equation for blessing that sets you up for unrealistic and unbiblical expectations? It goes something like this:

My obedience (Cause) → Yields God's blessing (Effect)

This sounds easy and predictable. All I needed to do was follow the rules and do my duty, and then God was going to pour out His favor, right? As a young adult I set my eyes on attaining the blessings of the basics—education, marital bliss, healthy kids, a nice house, and enough money to be comfortable. I wasn't greedy in my expectations, just sadly naive. Truly believing God's blessing to be defined in this way, I kept my head down, pressed forward and did my duty, determined to live my life as other nice church people indicated they were living. After all, if their message was correct, then blessing and prosperity were the result of mere cause and effect, and I was set to attain it.

But I was incredibly mistaken. The equation is false. We cannot reduce God's blessings to a formula that explains His way and workings in an individual life. I desperately needed awakened by the clarity of truth. And in his love, God would begin knocking on the door of my heart through the messenger of adversity.

Thankfully, I realize now that not only was the formula bad theology, it was completely housed in the small-minded package of self-determination and our own definition of what normal should be. I had been much like Tolkien's hobbits, Frodo and Sam of *The Lord of the Rings*. I was merely striving to create a life in the tranquility and safety of the Shire, which in and of itself was not a bad thing. It was the norm of most of Christians around me. Yet it required very little faith and very little desperation for God. Can you relate?

I would come to learn that normal, by human definition, isn't God's goal for any of us. After all, His glory made manifest in a human is far from ordinary. I began to see that living the abundant life Jesus talked about was sadly uncommon among the Christians I knew. Life abundant was something extraordinary, exceeding that which meets the eye and unavailable through self-effort, no matter how sincere. Finding it was going to require a departure from the status quo, even if it was the mindset of some very nice people.

Over the years, the process of awakening to greater expectations in my Christian journey included many uninvited and unexpected events. I would have never chosen certain circumstances God allowed in my life. I personally prefer to foresee the evil and avoid it. I'm not much of a natural risk-taker, so in the name of being prudent, it was easy to fall into a pattern of self-control rather than surrender to God.

But God, being God, has a better vantage point for how all things will work together for my good and His glory. In His love and omniscience He sought to increase my faith through events that He allowed to play out in my life story. He started with the raw material of a girl with limited vision and understanding, but whose heart was intentionally seeking *all* truth throughout the good, the bad and the ugly of life.

I remember when God began drawing my heart to Him for His strength and wisdom through my first unplanned, life-changing event. I was twenty years old and His story of grace commenced in very tangible ways as I buried my first baby. It continued to be written as He refined my faith and clarified my vision over the next twenty-five years. Through the deepest of disappointments in my first marriage, Jesus continually redirected my focus to His sufficiency in the face of unmet human expectations.

Awakening required the dream of a simple life in my own Shire to slowly crumble as my perceived control over the plot of my life was stripped away year after year. A shallow understanding of God and my relationship with Him was transformed as He accessed deeper and deeper layers of my heart, enabling me to experience more and more of His perfect love.

I've found that we can never predict how, out of the rubble of our smaller dream something much greater will be born when the pieces are surrendered to God. The birth of enlightenment for me was only through a life story

> We can never predict how, out of the rubble of our smaller dream something much greater will be born when the pieces are surrendered to God.

I had not planned. Just as it was for Tolkien's hobbits in their story, it is in mine: the pain endured, while taking this once-upon-a-time journey, produced a deep satisfaction and peace within my soul.

And you can have this fulfillment as well.

We each are part of a greater epic… a story that matters…a tale of an abundant life and great expectations. But as with every great story, there is an antagonist. We have an enemy who wants to deceive, distract, and destroy all of it, if we allow. My heart's desire is that you too are on your own journey to a more enlightened and abundant life. But I will warn you, enlightenment is birthed only through the painful decent into a tunnel of darkness—a path ultimately leading you to greater light.

First Things First: The Original Good versus Evil Story

We first must discover the truth about the context of this adventure we call life. For us to ever make sense of our life, especially in seasons when circumstances crush us, we must understand the truth about the ultimate beginning of the story. I'm referring to the link that ties everything in the middle to the end, a connection to the original once-upon-a-time factor. Embracing the full implication of this seemingly simple but complex truth will change your perspective, but only if you're looking. So here it is:

Once upon a time—also worded, *"In the beginning, God created the heavens and the earth."* (Genesis 1:1)

Yes, there you have it. The beginning. But what does this have to do with my life you may ask? Everything.

To establish the context for today, it is critical that we start in the beginning with the story of creation. Perhaps like me, you too began hearing this story at a very young age somewhere in basement Sunday school rooms. With small knees bumping into small feet, children gathered on blue carpet, big eyes glued to the flannel graph board. The teacher brought the story to life, telling of all God's handiwork as listed day by day in Genesis chapter one. Flannel images built the drama as the trees and flowers were added…then the sun and moon…the fish and the animals—and finally Adam and Eve.

It was such a good story. I had no trouble believing it and never doubted it. But it certainly did not seem personally applicable to me. I mean really, creation was a very, very

11

long time ago; the beginning was pretty remote. And so I filed this story with all of the other Bible stories explaining what I then believed to be a powerful but distant God who might zap me if I got out of line.

Thankfully, I was naively wrong about God and the significance creation has on my life. The story of God's loving creative power, impacting space and time according to His will and purpose, has everything to do with you and me. It provides the complete context for our lives. His handiwork didn't only unveil heaven and earth. He determined His image would be showcased through the first man and woman who were created for relationship with Him. After millennia of human generations, He still desires to manifest His same creative power in you and me. His image is to be made known through a relationship with us.

God had a plan: He created. And as we read in scripture, He did it perfectly.[1] But there is more to the story, and this is where the entire context for life comes into full view. It turns out as I learned much later, God had earlier created some things not detailed in Genesis chapter one.

One of them, called the anointed cherub, Lucifer, decided he was far too beautiful to be stuck in a support role. He no longer wished to be in the number two position under the authority of God, and so staged a coup. Discontent, Lucifer, determined to exist outside of all that was intended for him within the context of God's authority.

Bad choice.

As you can imagine, it didn't go well for him. We learn in Revelation 12:7-9 that he and his evil horde were kicked out of heaven, causing a major uproar as they were hurled down to the existing earth. Chaos ensued, hence Genesis 1:2. Darkness entered a once perfect universe, and the fight was on. The kingdom of darkness and the kingdom light were at war. Good versus evil battled and all of creation still groans, awaiting the final rescue.

And the power struggle between God and Lucifer beginning with that cataclysmic conflict over Lucifer's attempt to upstage God didn't end there. Lucifer, with a name meaning, "Light-Bearer," became the one who obscures the Light. He perpetuates darkness in our current world—*even within our own stories.*

Your Story Belongs within the Context of His

Despite the chaotic resistance within the universe, God's divine plan continued to progress. He created mankind to have dominion over the earth and to expand the nature and manifestation of His own glory.[2] Man and woman in perfect communion with their Creator became bearers of His Light. They were clothed by God's own glory and had utmost value and purpose. No corruption or pain tainted their world. No disease or heartache. No disappointment or regret.

But, as you know perfection on the earth would not last for long. God's enemy was not fond of the restorative replacement plan and plotted to destroy the beauty of God's creative expression. The battle between Light and darkness prevailed.

You've likely heard how the conflict continued to unfold with the account found in Genesis. Satan initiated his strategy by targeting the woman. He deceived Eve by getting her to doubt God's credibility and soon, along with Adam, they found themselves doing the one thing they had been commanded not to do.

Then everything changed in an instant. Their glorious and abundant normal was irrevocably altered. A bad choice ushered in chaos and confusion. They had decided to step outside the context of God's authority to do life on their own terms. Does this sound slightly familiar?

Thankfully, God in His love and omniscience was still on His throne. He had a plan to provide an eventual happy ending to the long saga and would defeat darkness by the power of His light, the Light of the world.[3] While we might think we would have done it differently, He knew that the free will He had given Lucifer, and then again to mankind, is the only access point by which to experience authentic, true relationship with His creation. We were purposefully designed with the capacity to choose a relationship with Him—or choose against Him.

Because God is love,[4] He wants a real relationship of love born out of desire, not based upon mandated, robotic, task-oriented duty. Our powerful ability to choose became part of His plan for eternity.

A plan that includes you.

A plan that includes me.

A plan that allows us to choose truth in the midst of a broken and chaotic world.

I hope, as God does, that you've already chosen to be part of the greatest story ever told. Your tale can be part of the epic romance of the ages. It's the divinely inspired saga beginning with a loving Creator who is seek-

> Your tale can be part of the epic romance of the ages.

ing to either initiate or strengthen a relationship with you. God desires your awakening. He yearns to give you clarity, a full-awareness enabling you to partner with Him in fulfilling the purpose He's written on your heart. It's only in doing so that we will exceed normal and thrive, finally living the abundant life.

We must become aware of the immutable link joining The Beginning to our own Here and Now. And regrettably, this depth of understanding is uncommon, both among the churched and unchurched alike. To build a framework for a lucid life story, however; we must first grasp our personal and real connection back to our Creator. The tragedy of failing to make this connection thwarts our comprehension of our true identity and purpose. And these two issues, the content of much we will explore in later chapters, are like points on a vector establishing the trajectory of our lives. Without personally understanding our essential relationship with God, we misunderstand who we are and why we are here. Thus confusion becomes our norm.

But this does not have to describe your story. You have a choice, just as I did.

You can defy the chaos.

You can choose the deviance of clarity.

And you can exceed.

Freedom in Truth or False-Security in Ignorance

If you want set free to thrive, the first foundational truth to grasp is this: *you have immense value and purpose—* no matter what's happened in your life and despite what others may have told you. *God intentionally created you to be you. He loves you for who you are, just as you are, and He has a plan.* But just like way back in the beginning, darkness in the character of Satan seeks to prevail against the light of God. He attempts to cloud your vision of the truth and lead you to the wrong choices.

The opportunity to thrive, living a fulfilled life of purpose in connection to our Creator and in authentic community with others, is possible through a relationship with Jesus Christ. It's a simple choice. You can live a life story of impact and leave an eternal legacy. You can have peace in the midst of the chaos. But how can we do this when the world, and ours in particular, seems to be falling apart?

The key is tied to your understanding of context.

As you continue to ponder the beginning and how the truth of God's larger plan is intersecting your life, perhaps you're being challenged with an entirely new paradigm. It may be that you feel a bit like Neo, the main character in the 1999 film, *The Matrix*.

In the course of his story, Neo is offered a choice. Only one option would give him the opportunity to discover the truth of his existence and provide the context for truly living his purpose. The appeal of one option, the blue pill, is blissful ignorance. He could remain falsely secure in a fictitious and futile reality, continuing to live the normal life as one of the masses. As an oblivious captive, he could cling to the illusion while going through the motions of life without purpose or impact.

But there was an alternative to consider. The red pill of truth.

It was the truth transcending the normal, usurping what seemed to be, and offering an awakening to an enhanced reality. For us, this transcendent truth is available through God's grace. We have an unmerited opportunity, but even as it was for Neo, the implications of the truth's power make it dangerous. A predatory enemy strategically attempts to destroy or obscure our new clarity at every turn.

We can choose the truth and enter a new dimension to discover and fulfill our destiny. We don't have to stay captive to the norm of diversionary chaos and ignorance. We can opt out of the bondage of our self-limiting thought patterns and unhealthy relational habits.

The chaos in my story, with all the disappointment, discouragement and disillusionment, was skillfully used by God to awaken me. But it could have easily accomplished the enemy's agenda had I not chosen all of the truth. And all of the truth required me to look into the darkest and deepest recesses of my heart and deal with what would be revealed. Deceit told me it wasn't worth the hassle or the pain, but I am here to tell you, it is.

The truth set me free from lies that could have kept me captive. I chose to exceed the status quo by believing the truth of God's Word for all areas of my life in the here-and-now. I wanted to be set free to thrive.

And God longs to do the same for you, if you're willing. Are you?

Your Choice—Choose Truth

Only by making an intentional choice to be different, to be unplugged from the matrix of chaos, will you fulfill your full destiny. Consciously choosing to co-author the tale of your life in the context the Creator designed is the key. We all have the opportunity to live a story of real life, the abundant life in the midst of battle, equipped with the power to stand in victory.

And while this exceeds the "normal" life, and is certainly not easy, it is one of transcendent peace and clarity. It's a life where heartache and hardship remain, but when viewed through God's grace, yields unexplainable joy. It was the choice I began making on that December day when the last remnants of my dreams came crashing in around me. I refused to allow the sting of life's circumstances to define my present and destroy my future.

I implore you to make the same decision for yourself.

The first step is to choose God's truth in its unabridged entirety. You must commit to apply your discoveries to the way you think about God, the way you view yourself, and your relationships with others. Uncommon clarity and peace in this world of chaos can be yours if you desire. But then again, you can also choose to get plugged back in to ignorance, eat a bag of chips and watch reality TV to dull the pain and escape the emptiness.

Remember, you have options because our loving Creator gave us the capacity of choice.

Life or death?

Light or darkness?

Liberty or captivity?

Truth or deception?

Do you feel the divine discontent, a longing for deeper meaning in life? Do you yearn for truth and the freedom that knocks at the door of your soul? You'll be unsatisfied until the deeper desire is acknowledged.

So go ahead—choose truth…and all of it.

Exceed normal and escape the prison of confusion.

I'll see you outside the bars, finally free and fully alive.

KEYS TO THRIVE

Choose Truth.

1) What is it about truth that makes it difficult for people to accept? *Truth requires responsibility & action*

2) Have you ever been tempted to use denial as a coping mechanism rather than seeking the whole truth? *yes*

3) What are the benefits and the costs of using denial as a coping mechanism? *benefits - immediate gratification costs long term cheater*

4) Ponder the statement, "Enlightenment to the truth shatters our delusion of control." Why are we as humans so desperate to live within our delusion of control? *It makes us feel like we can determine our outcome*

5) Truth to ponder: John 3:17-21; John 14:6; John 17:17; Ephesians 4:21; 2 Timothy 2:15

2

THE FOG OF WAR

Why Does Chaos Shroud Your Tale?

I hate war as only a soldier who has lived it can.
Yet one thing can be said to its credit.
Victory required a mighty manifestation of the
most ennobling virtues of man.
Faith. Courage. Fortitude. Sacrifice.

General Dwight D. Eisenhower, June 10, 1946

M y dad was a soldier, although I don't remember him as such. He was drafted into the United States Army in early 1963 as part of the military build-up during the Vietnam era. I was never identified as an "army brat," and our family was spared from the inconveniences involved with that difficult but noble career. Instead, he did his duty and was honorably discharged. A military lifestyle ended for me before my second birthday. But nevertheless, over time a military mindset and awareness would grow.

My interest in real-life, real-time war was heightened to new levels when my nineteen-year-old son decided to give five years of his life to the United States Marine Corps. The blood of Americans seeped into the sand of faraway places, leaving an indelible mark on the souls of those who fought with them, as well as in the hearts of their loved ones. My tears, like those of countless other mothers, soaked carpet and stained the pages of our open Bibles as we engaged the assault in a different dimension.

I chose to be fully engaged emotionally and spiritually in a distant war raging physically because I was aware of the danger. I knew there was an openly hostile, yet devious enemy seeking to destroy my son and his comrades. And to make it more urgent and grievous, I knew of the inner battle my son was fighting as the enemy of his soul attempted to gain a foothold.

I ached to "do" something but was getting a personal lesson on how battles of eternal value were to be won or lost. I couldn't physically participate in urban warfare, kicking in doors, and driving out a physical enemy with a shower of bullets—but I could still fight. And so that's what I did.

The Context of War

Something fierce resides within my soul. Does it in yours? Beneath the reserved exterior is something one might not expect, something tough as nails. It's a relentless warrior's heart, determining long-ago that failure is not an option. It's a heart that presses forward, no matter the setbacks and despite the chaos that seeks to shroud all that is good and beautiful in life.

My desire to fight against the evil and chaos surrounding my son was driven by something I had experienced previously during times of great adversity beyond my control. Battling cycles of abandonment, trying to be strong for the sake of the children, and functioning practically as a single parent is an emotional, spiritual and physical struggle for many. No matter what type of pain or tactics of hardship we endure, I've noted a similar theme: the enemy cloaks his work in the fog of war.

Consequently, our position as warriors in the midst of a chaotic battlefield must be consistently understood. We are to keep the lines of communication open to the command center, the throne room of God, asking for protective reinforcements to be sent to the front line.

Resolve and faith are tested in the fires of adversity. And while thankfully, I've never been forced to put on a kevlar vest and go into physical combat, I've learned to use a piece of military equipment known as the shield of faith. My eyes haven't personally seen the horrors of flesh torn apart by the weapons of war, but my life and my heart still bear the scars of war. And I'll bet yours does too.

The sooner we grasp this essential truth, the more prepared we can be: all of life is lived in the context of war. Every. Single. Day. Of. It. Clear and convincing threats have been identified. Comrades have fallen in the battle. And while

> All of life is lived in the context of war. Every. Single. Day. Of. It.

the norm may be to mind your own business, speak with political expediency, smile, and keep your head down, we must choose to engage in the fight that wars against us. Together we must advance the mission, thriving as we manifest faith, courage, fortitude and sacrifice.

But there's something we must work through before we can hope to successfully advance any mission of value.

It's blindness.

Personal desensitization.

Comfortable captivity.

The context of war is frequently unrecognized or unacknowledged in any relevant way within Christian circles. In fact, some have been captives of war for so long, the will to fight has all but been beaten out of them. Living as defeated prisoners controlled by opposition forces, they've blindly surrendered. Many live in their personal Shire, desensitized to evil, and oblivious to their captivity.

Prisoners of War

Mental, emotional and spiritual bondage is the norm of far too many people who claim to know Christ. Sadly, some live chaotic and defeated lives in a camp spiritually controlled by the enemy. Oppressed and intimidated by fear, doubt and dejection, most would admit at one time they had hoped to thrive and live a life of impact. A desire to leave a lasting legacy was once the dream, but cords cinched tightly by the consequence of past decisions and present circumstances leave them feeling trapped. Senses dulled by the constant propaganda of chaos, prisoners are reduced to mere survival tactics. With hearts now mostly dead to the pain, they simply go through the motions of life.

I've found one common factor among far too many people—*real vision is often shrouded.* And without vision based in *full* reality, thoughts become confused and disjointed. The battles fought on the turf of our hearts bring us to a point of decision. We can stand in the ultimate freedom our Commander has already won, or we can give up, only to be captured and tormented by the enemy.

Real vision, with our eyes open to the true nature of our potential captors, is critical. Without it we risk succumbing to a spiritual version of the Stockholm Syndrome. This is the phenomenon when our affections become wrongfully attached to those imprisoning us, our allegiance blindly aligned with the cause of our enemy—even to the point of fighting against our own rescue.

> Spiritual Stockholm Syndrome manifests as wrong attachments and blind allegiance to the cause of our enemy.

It's important to remember we are part of the epic war of the ages between good and evil…between order and chaos…between purpose and futility. There is no way to avoid it. War is individually private but common to all. And it's in the battlefield of your mind that you will either overcome confusion and take control of your thoughts, or be overwhelmed as the destroyer obscures your vision with his barrage of lies and accusations.

Satan knows better than we do: "*Without vision, the people perish*." (Proverbs 29:18)

The Fog of War: An Adversary's Tactile Advantage

We all can feel a bit, or perhaps very confused for a very real reason. Sadly, a prevailing fog continues to disorient many people, including Christians, who are doing the best they can with what they know. This fog clouds our vision and causes us to lose focus. The chaos keeps coming and many do well to put one foot in front of the other. As with all military strategies, the longer the fog of war goes unrecognized, the greater the damage to be sustained.

The fog of war is a recognized military concept pre-emptively studied by world military leaders and attributed to Carl Von Clausewitz's famous 1832 treatise, *On War*. It's the barrier to effective decision-making in military operations, resulting from lack of a clear state of mind and lack of information. Without clarity, the precision necessary for success becomes unattainable in the volatility, uncertainty and complexity of war.[1]

Are you beginning to see the applicability of this issue in our daily lives? Military leaders go to War College to learn how to proactively combat the detrimental effects of confusion on leadership decision-making and on the troops. You and I must study the fog of war from a spiritual perspective to counter its confusing effects in our lives.

Uncertainty and doubt are classic messengers of our enemy. We've all experienced them. At first the enemy distracts with ease by clouding the Christian's mind to the concept of war. Then he causes us to feel doubtful about our capability while shrouding his nature and intent. Lastly, he minimizes our situational awareness, causing hesitation at the very least and at the worst, paralysis due to fear.

Satan is a master strategist. He leads the warrior to be tentative, either because of doubt or due to a failure to know his or her mission. He keeps us hesitant and timid... wavering...easily tossed to and fro and scared in the midst of the battle. Satan keeps many among the ranks completely uncertain of whom they really are and ashamed of what they believe they're not.

> Satan keeps many among the ranks completely uncertain of whom they really are and ashamed of what they believe they're not.

Tragically, keeping you uncertain about your identity keeps you soft and prevents you from developing into the warrior you are intended to be. He delights in the one dimensional and surface-deep conversations and relationships among Christians. He encourages emotionally driven decision making and takes away your ability to critically think.

In fact, the devil has done a masterful job, even in the Christian community, to spread the lie that critically thinking and evaluating incoming data is to sinfully judge. Just as he did with Eve, he easily twists what we thought we knew of God's Word. He's led people to believe that to judge, which is *to evaluate the evidence*, is a sin. He knows most will never review the context of the scripture to discover the full truth, and disarms the warrior without a fight.

Satan also uses pampering propaganda to shroud his adversarial intent. In Western developed countries such as the United States, "God wants me to be happy" is the mantra. Even among Christians, personal pleasure, recreation and having fun is the priority—not sober-minded thinking and personal consecration. The frenzy of life drains us and entitled spirits lead us to reward ourselves with whatever our form of pleasure may be. The enemy doubles over with laughter at the ease with which he wins this battle. Idols of entertainment, hedonism, and self firmly reign in Christian and non-Christian homes alike. Unsuspecting victims never notice that he cleverly shrouded their awareness to any war.

Are you beginning to understand how your real purpose as a warrior has become thwarted by the smoke screen of the enemy? The kingdom of darkness takes ground and the church shakes its head in disbelief about what is happening "out there." But those free to thrive know what's out there is regrettably "in here."

Sadly distracted, nice church-people claiming to be Christians are many times unaware. "Out there" is only a reflection of "in here." While we were redeemed to be soldiers, it

> It is in the comfortable captivity of oblivion that we've become prisoners of war.

is in the comfortable captivity of oblivion that we've become prisoners of war. Until each of us recognize, "in here" actually translates to "in me," the effects of the fog of war will prevail. We have been commanded to be the salt and light in our world. But our enemy is a skilled proponent of darkness and knows how to chain us with confusion.

Consequently, we must be intentional and study the adversary's strategy and tactics to recognize and then overcome his ploys. Strategic military victory is the outcome of deliberate and intentional training, planning and execution.

Fogging Your Mind: A Three-Pronged Strategy

Jesus, in John 10:10, clearly warns of the enemy's threefold intent as contrasted to his own abundant plan and purpose for our lives.

> *"The thief does not come except to steal, and to kill, and to destroy. I have come that they may have life, and that they may have it more abundantly."*

Three deliberate and malicious prongs to the hook of Satan's modus operandi are revealed. Steal. Kill. Destroy. In this verse Jesus highlights how the enemy approaches us first—as a thief. He's watched Satan's subtle strategy on humans since the Garden. Let's go back to Eden to investigate. From the earliest campaign against mankind and their Creator we see a striking pattern emerge. The same three-pronged plan Jesus warns of in John, is first used by Satan in Genesis 3:1-5.

Here he asks Eve, *"Has God indeed said, 'You shall not eat of every tree of the garden?'"* A simple question, was it not? But the adversary is a practiced manipulator and never seeks out a casual encounter for no purpose. In fact, his question was masterfully framed to set the first hook in his plan to destroy Adam and Eve. He uses the same ploy on us as well.

Steal

The devil purposefully left out one highly important word in the question to Eve about God's original message found in Genesis 2:16. The couple had been told they may eat of every tree "*freely*," except for the tree of the knowledge of good and evil.

Freely eat.

In *abundance*. Without lack.

But our adversary knew the word "freely," was a vital word and concept to steal. He had to get Eve to doubt the loving, benevolent nature of God. It was through this tactic that Satan stole the very thing God wanted to lavish on mankind, and that which Jesus explains He came to give: life *abundant*. Satan skillfully reframed the reference to God to infer a deficiency. He directed Eve's mind to perceive a lack. He stole abundance, and in the process swept away clarity without her suspecting a thing until it was too late.

With a misguided focus on what we "don't have" we are unable to clearly see all we have been given by our loving God. Instead of living with confidence, we entertain doubt. This fog triggers discontent and our ability to trust God is challenged as the framework of our faith is assaulted. Faith, the foundation of our relationship with God, begins to crumble when we fail to take control of thoughts doubting God's Word and His goodness. The downward spiral begins.

Kill

The second prong of Satan's three-pronged hook takes hold through another masterful misquote of God's word. This time it's from Eve, herself.

> *"We may eat of the fruit of the trees of the garden: But of the fruit of the tree which is in the midst of the garden, God has said, 'You shall not eat of it, nor shall you touch it, lest you die.'"* (Genesis 2:2-3)

With the first prong of stolen abundance established, Eve compounds her problem by not correcting Satan's original misquote. She now unwisely adds her own flair to God's word: *"nor shall you touch it."* With her focus on deficiency, she overstated her responsibility, adding a restrictive burden God never intended. She played right into the enemy's hand by focusing on perceived scarcity. This mindset coupled with a self-imposed burden targeted her hope in God, just as it does to ours.

Life in general gets much more difficult when placing unnecessary or unrealistic expectations on ourselves and others, does it not? Self-imposed expectations leave us disappointed, dejected and discouraged. Vitality is drained and often we incorrectly blame God while dying a slow death entrenched in the victim-mindset. Jesus invites us to rest in Matthew 11:28-30. He promises we will find rest unto our souls because His burden is light. But bearing burdens not intended for us causes discouragement over time, killing our hope.

The victim mindset reveals a fogged mind and makes us easy targets. Satan wants to slowly bleed us spiritually, laughing as we die an excruciating death while wrongly believing we are helpless to do anything about it. His deceit leads to emotional exhaustion.

He whispers that we must live up to other people's expectations and maintain a certain image. He discourages us by pointing out our own fleshly inadequacies and the failures of others. He ushers in doubt who sneeringly asserts: "You can't hope in the goodness of God! After all, if God is so good, why is your life so challenging and such a disappointment? Why have people hurt or betrayed you? Why can't you measure up to others? You need to try harder!"

Once discouragement has a foothold, the fog of despair, or hopelessness, will not be far behind. Becoming hopeless can also be described as "losing heart." We are prone to lose heart in tough and drawn-out chapters in our stories. This is why we must view life in its proper context, learn to survey the battlefield, and resist the enemy's strategies.

> Hopelessness stops our beating hearts emotionally and shrouds our spiritual sight.

Allowing ourselves to become hopeless is fatal. Have you ever noticed that eventually the acute pain of disappointment stops and oddly, at some point, you simply don't care anymore? If the pain wasn't dealt with properly, your heart will have become hardened as the outcome of hopelessness set in.

Apathy.

It manifests as a lack of interest or desire. Apathetic people have no concern for others and in many cases, no hopeful enthusiasm for life. If apathetic, the fog of chaos may swirl around a person, but they no longer care. "So what," you say. "Whatever," you shrug. And the voice in your head continues to whisper something like this: "There is no point in caring. If you don't expect anything, you can't get disappointed."

When our soul is weary and our heart is deadened we cannot live with vigor. We become too anemic and weak as soldiers to execute our God-given purpose. In fact, in our apathetic state we find we may not even care about anything other than surviving another day, doing it our own way. Consider the words the Israelites spoke to the prophet Jeremiah when he exhorted them for their apathetic state:

"...There is no hope: but we will walk after our own devices, and we will everyone do the imagination of his evil heart." (Jeremiah 18:12)

They had given up. No hope. Essentially they told God, "We have no hope in you so will do whatever we feel like doing and live the way we want." When our spiritual health degenerates to this point our status is critical. Our enemy is killing us.

The progression of Satan's strategy is clear and I hope you see it. Our enemy begins his methodical and evil work in our lives as a thief. First, he will steal your faith in the goodness of God's intent for abundance in your life. Next, he will seek the slaughter by bleeding you of your heart's life-sustaining force, hope. He is then poised with the third and final prong of his hook, plotting to sink it deeply for your destruction.

Destroy

In true fashion of a liar, Satan misguided Eve's focus again, further clouding the clarity of God's Word to set the final prong of his destructive strategy.

"And the serpent said unto the woman, 'You will not surely die: For God knows that in the day you eat of it your eyes

will be opened, and you will be like God, knowing good and evil.'" (Genesis 3:4-5, *NKJV*)

Here Satan gets bold, blatantly contradicting God. Audaciously he denies God's word as relevant and complete for her life, casting doubt on God's *intentions*. He convinces her she is a fool to trust God's purpose and design for her life. Satan then plants the toxic thought that God is withholding something good from her.

Her thoughts began to swirl as do ours in these moments of attack. "I could have so much more… I could have it all…why won't God give me this?" She feels betrayed and ignorant. How could God do this to her, and how could she have been so blind?

Satan's desire is to cause Eve to believe she is defenseless against a God who is holding out on her. "Rise up, take matters into you own hands. You need to protect yourself," the serpent hissed. And with diabolical glee he embedded the last prong of his fatal hook. "Destroy!" was the chant heard among the powers of darkness, echoing even today.

Let's take a deeper look at what's transpiring. In Jesus' warning to us in John 10:10, the Greek word translated in English "to destroy" conveys the meaning *"to render useless."*[2] All creation groaned when that third hook sunk deep into the heart of mankind. In arrogant delight Satan sneered in the face of God as the swirl of wicked chaos began to encompass God's beautiful crowning jewel of creation. God's darling, Eve, had been destroyed and on her heels was Adam. Created in God's image and for His glory, *Eve had been designed to give life, but was now rendered useless to fulfill her mission to do so.*

However, you will note that her destruction was not complete annihilation. Eve didn't suddenly fail to exist. Rather, destruction was the state of becoming useless for the purpose created. Her mission was destroyed when she took matters into her own hands. By refusing to rest in her God-ordained design to magnify His glory, Eve opened herself up to destruction, just as we do today. She attempted to deify herself with her desire to "become like God."

> By refusing to rest in her God-ordained design to magnify His glory, Eve opened herself up to destruction, just as we do today.

Death was ushered in with her misguided attempts at self-preservation. By failing to trust God's Word and by refusing to rest in His goodness, she allowed Satan's destructive strategy to confuse her, trap her—and the rest is history.

Implications for Life

Life with real purpose, which requires connecting to God and others in authenticity, becomes impossible when attempting to protect and promote ourselves. As we've seen, Satan is a thief, but he is so much more. Jesus clearly outlined the evil strategy to destroy us. Our enemy experiences great satisfaction when Christians live unknowingly as victims. Instead of living as victors, too many go through the motions, living in practical faithlessness.

Our belief in the power that works within us must be exercised by intentional action if we are to be victorious in the battles we face. People who say they have faith in Jesus to eternally save them from their sins, but who live this life in apathetic resignation are prisoners of war. The key to escape is believing and then acting upon the truth of Jesus Christ's supremacy over Satan, refusing to be a casualty of war.

But blindly, and out of fear and lack of knowledge, many nice church people invest their energy in image management activities to cover their inner defeat. Rather than finding fulfillment in being who they are designed to be as image bearers of Christ and warriors for His cause, they become comfortable captives. Some are in blissful ignorance while others are apathetic, but many are imprisoned, their minds fogged with deceit and distraction. They are unable to live in intimacy with Christ, thus incapacitated to execute their God-ordained purpose.

But it doesn't have to be like this.

The bars of the enemy's prison camp once held me. My vision had been fogged and in the midst of doing my Christian duty I believed that my hurting heart was a personal weakness that proved I was inferior. I didn't recognize that the pain was actually a symptom of a wound I needed to take to Jesus for healing. Instead, I learned to play the image management game because that's what "strong Christians" with "strong faith" did. I kept trying harder but felt like a failure—a disappointment to God. Sure, I knew, at least in my head, He loved me…but I believed He did not love me quite as much as His other kids.

The sin that had trapped me was my belief in the lie that God's love was conditional and based on my performance. Because I had agreed with the enemy, a piece of my heart was chained up, subject to his evil control.

Satan's deceit kept me from the deeper connection God wanted with me, the kind of abiding intimacy necessary for true victory through Christ. So out of His love, He allowed the hardships of life to lead me on a journey to a place of complete dependence. A place I would come to recognize as entrance to the freedom I'd been missing.

Your Choice—Stand in Freedom

It is an intentional decision to rise up and operate with the confidence and clarity Jesus offers for a life of freedom. We have been given eternal life and hope as followers of Jesus Christ. Our identity is secure. Our purpose is established. The victory has been won despite the enemy continuing to pummel our mind with lies.

The truth of scripture teaches that we are fully equipped and empowered to partake in God's divine nature, which is one of absolute and authoritative supremacy and unwavering victory. (2 Peter 2:1-5) But to take part in God's nature and His victory, we must allow Him to live through us. This is only possible when *we die to ourselves and surrender to the Spirit of God within us*. We'll be covering more on how to get to this point in subsequent chapters.

We are enabled to execute our divine purpose and advance His redemptive plan only when we learn to depend solely on Him. We are to be life givers and light bearers created in the image of God, reflecting His Glory on this earth as we stand in His strength. But this means choosing to defy the confusion found in the comfortable captivity of the status quo, which tends to include a lot of fear-based self-protection.

Don't allow the enemy's fog of war to devour the impact of your life through his three-pronged strategy to steal, kill, and destroy. Your life story is not intended to be consumed in bondage.

Stand victorious in the battle through the power of Christ in you.

Refuse captivity as a prisoner of war; choose freedom and exceed in life.

You are a warrior. Now rise to stand.

KEYS TO THRIVE

Stand in Freedom.

1) In your life personally, what have been the greatest barriers to standing in spiritual and emotional freedom so that you can live fully? *fear of what He will ask, fear of my ability to*

2) Have you received Christ as your Savior and Lord, claiming the freedom He offers? (Review Romans 5:8-11; Romans 10:9-10 &13; John 8:32) *Yes*

3) Has the enemy of your soul stolen your joy or peace? *joy at times*

4) Are you ready to learn to fight back? Becoming a warrior requires obedience to the Commander, submission to His training program, and commitment to His mission.

5) Truth to ponder: 2 Timothy 2:3-4; Romans 8:37; Galatians 5:1; Ephesians 6:14

3

LET THERE BE LIGHT

Are You Ready for a Change?

New life delivered through grace,
New joy transcending the pain,
Divine design revealed through suffering,
Surrendered to the Sovereign,
I am free.

Kaye Carter, 2012

Over the years I have come to realize there is a certain cadence to the strategies of the battle warring against our souls. Circumstances differ and details vary, but common tactics are waged against us all. It was a sunny day in May when I first became acutely aware of the battle seeking to engulf me. I was twenty years old and had been married just over two months. Busily, I had worked to finish my sophomore year in nursing school, completing finals the week prior.

I was happily looking forward to a summer break with my high-school sweetheart and husband. Expecting our first baby was going to present its share of challenges over the coming months, but I was happy and content, full of hope for all life had to offer in the future, mesmerized by the illusion of my own expectation.

When he suddenly left me for the first of what would be many times, it was not part of a story I had planned. He declared with icy cool that he did not want to be married anymore, leaving our small apartment without explanation and stranding me without a car. Waves of fear and confusion washed over me. The shock and anger came later, like a tsunami overwhelming my mind with the impact of abandonment.

I did not have the clarity at the time to label it a betrayal, but knew it was a major pot hole on the road to a life of the happily ever-after. Chaotic thoughts and confusion fogged my mind as I tried to make meaning out of what was occurring. There had been no argument the night before. There was no crisis to lead him to this conclusion. Maybe he was just immature. Maybe he was just overwhelmed with the impending responsibilities and financial concern. Out of pure love I tried every which way to excuse his poor behavior as I refused to allow myself to be enveloped in the darkness of doubt and depression that can come at a time of disillusionment.

After a week and a "talking-to" from my father, he came back claiming he was sorry. Regrettably, over the coming years it would become clear that his sorrow was not true repentance as the evidence of his own bondage mounted. In that moment, however, I was naively ecstatic, just relieved he was back.

When the baby girl came premature and physically defective, the war against my soul intensified and refused to be ignored. This time, compounded by more bad theology, punitive visions of God contributed to more chains binding my heart. Sadly, my misguided perceptions added false-but-seemingly-real credibility to the voices of darkness.

The voices sneeringly told me that God was punishing me as a result of premarital sin. Despite regret and true repentance, the voices claimed I was bad and God was mad. The life of my child was the price for my wayward act. Doubt and shame tormented my insecure and fearful soul. They convinced me that I was only worthy of chaos and emptiness; I deserved a broken, useless, unhappy life...although if I was smart, I'd better pretend my life was just fine.

Crushed by the death of my tiny daughter, my shattered hopes and dreams were buried along with her broken body on a sweltering August day. The heat and humidity intensified the overwhelming weight of my sorrow, constricting my throat as I repressed the primal cry welling up from deep within. A draped row of folding chairs arranged upon artificial green turf faced a tiny white casket. I sat before it and the searing pain of a mother's sorrow tore me apart internally. Externally, however, I maintained the appearance of calm by forcing my focus on delicate pink, cascading roses. Their beauty attempted to camouflage the sum representation of sin's emptiness and ugliness: death.

A story that was supposed to end with a happily ever-after was over before it barely started. My baby would never grow up. The blanket I'd stitched would go unused. *My expectation had delivered something defective.* Handicapped. Flawed and short-lived. Why...why? Was there a purpose? Why was I being singled out for punishment when I personally knew of so many other Christians around me who "got away" with the same sin? Was God arbitrary or was I just especially bad?

I struggled to breathe and felt the perspiration trickle down my back while the preacher in the black suit appropriately said whatever there is to say in these moments. I was present but absent. I wanted to run but could not. The madness and the oppressive cords were winding themselves around my heart, submerging my mind in darkness and despair. I felt trapped, but knew no way out. The three-pronged strategy of the enemy was effectively stealing… killing…and destroying me while I was unaware.

Unknown at the time, I had become a captive. The voice of chaos was gleefully having his way within me. Doubt was imprisoning my mind as I struggled with disillusionment and depression over the coming months. Shame and discouragement tormented me due to my incorrect interpretations of the wrath and the love of God. The liar had effectively convinced me that God's love was allotted according to some sort of scale. I grieved not only the death of my baby, but also the death of a dream for a story-book perfect life and the hope that I would ever measure up.

When the end of August came I didn't have the strength to go back to nursing school. I was too emotionally exhausted and spiritually adrift. I'd gone from a happy, albeit naive girl expecting so much from life, to becoming a woman with a scarred and broken heart. Disillusioned by pain, the evil voices disparaged and shamed me for the stupidity of believing I could have had anything different from what I got as a sinful, imperfect girl.

The well-meaning church-ladies quoted scripture about all things working out for the good, but of course, I knew they didn't know the whole story. In my head, the voice of condemnation loved to mockingly preach that I was "reaping what I had sown." I endured the ladies telling me I would have more children, as if that would take the place of the one I buried. I wanted to scream, but politely smiled. Alone in a fight I was ill-equipped to win, I had no one with whom I could "be real." Feeling forsaken, I cried an ocean of tears and learned to pretend I was much stronger than I was.

Oh, to be free from the suffocating stench of the war within and the death it perpetrated. I desired peace. I wanted pain to have some meaning. I yearned for clarity. And I didn't know it then, but what I needed was inner healing. I wish I could tell you it was soon thereafter that I found what I desired, but much more was to be written into my story on the journey to greater vision.

Let me stop now and check in with you: Can you relate to this journey? Not to the details of my story necessarily, but to the effects of pain from the unexpected, unplanned and unwanted events in your life? Can you relate to the effects of chaos and the overwhelming desire to be free from the power of confusion? Have you ever heard the lying voices in your head, discouraging you, condemning you, laughing at your plight and telling you it's hopeless to want more? Do you feel alone and trapped with a yearning to find meaning and clarity?

I wish I would have known earlier that the cadence of chaos is uncertainty and its voice is doubt. These two battle tactics are fiery darts effectively clouding the vision and binding the hearts of many Christians, young and old. It is the *eyes* of our heart for which our enemy regularly takes aim.

Satan knows that we are much less effective warriors without eyes to see reality. Without vision—people perish. Our enemy knows if he can blind you with uncertainty your defeat will readily affect many with whom you have contact. Somehow by God's Spirit I knew this and I kept begging for real vision, not understanding the route life would take to deliver the clarity I needed.

> It is the *eyes* of our heart for which our enemy regularly takes aim.

Open the Eyes of Your Heart

"My eye affects my heart," we read in Lamentations 3:51. Our focus is of utmost importance. Without clear sight we cannot live in the abundance Christ came to give. But passivity will not deliver it. Intentional action is required if we wish to ever experience God's full creative beauty and abundance. You will remember God eradicated the chaos recorded in Genesis with action and by His word.

> *"The spirit of God moved...and God said, 'let there be light, and there was light.'"* (Genesis 1:2-3)

Everything changed in that moment. All that had been without form, disorderly, obscured by chaos and darkness was now irrevocably altered by the movement and spoken word of the Creator. *"Let there be light."* They were powerful, focused words that established the theme for His entire story for the ages to come, including yours and mine. Contemplate this concept for a moment.

All God does from that point in the beginning—until now and through all future events to come—*is to intentionally advance his original creative and redemptive plan.* By lighting the darkness, God powerfully moved to set free His creation from the void of chaos. This includes our world of inner chaos. He would advance His creative plan in my life once I

> All God does from that point in the beginning—until now and through all future events to come—*is to intentionally advance his original creative and redemptive plan.*

learned to fully "let" there be Light, and He will do the same for you.

Required for vision both physically and spiritually, light delivers freedom from the prison of darkness. Without light in our lives, we may do the best we can to squint and strain, guessing what the menu for life reads like an over-forty-year-old patron in a dimly lit restaurant. It is impossible to know the options described with certainty unless the eyes are given more light. In like manner spiritually, without light in our lives, our perceptions are extremely limited. Our vision becomes indistinct and confused when shrouded in the darkness.

In this life, as in the restaurant, many times we hope for the best without asking for help, putting in our order despite lack of clarity. Looking forward to our chosen entree, we convince ourselves we did pretty well on our own. But our heart drops when it arrives. It is nothing as we expected.

Think about this on a spiritual level. We think we can see well enough spiritually at times, refusing to admit we need more light. When the details are revealed and the consequences of choices made by us and others become apparent, we become disillusioned, lamenting, "This is not what I expected!"

Focus your thoughts as you allow some light to penetrate your perceptions about moments of disillusionment in your own life. As I began to focus on what spiritually was occurring in my life at times of disappointment, the Light revealed a revolutionary perspective that changed my entire outlook on my war-torn life.

Our personal expectations are flawed due to clouded vision and lack of light; we are prone to believing an illusion. Disillusionment is therefore, inevitable. And while having our illusion stripped away may cause heartache, the acute pain can lead to eternal gain.

Perhaps this is a difficult pill to swallow, but I promise, it's true.

Disillusionment as the Gateway to Enlightenment

To be released from an illusion is to be freed from that which *deceives* by producing a *false or misleading impression of reality.* The acute pain of disillusionment is real no matter how we end up there. It never feels like a happy place. We feel a mixture of shame for our potential stupidity and we are angry with others or perhaps with God for our unfulfilled expectations. It catches us unaware. We don't usually see it coming until light is cast upon the object, person, or situation to reveal the reality we previously missed.

Why do we allow disillusionment to initiate a cascade of emotions leading to prolonged depression or perhaps even despair, instead of being grateful that we can now see reality? Many otherwise sane people I've encountered, actually prefer their fantasy over reality. They willfully choose ignorance and denial as protective mechanisms to deal with unwanted truth.

This applies even to some Christians. Living their story as modern day versions of the emperor, from the childhood story by Hans Christian Andersen, *The Emperor's New Clothes,* they surround themselves with people who will only tell them what they want to hear. But just as was exemplified in Andersen's story, *turning a blind eye to truth never changes its reality.* The emperor was exposed and vulnerable despite the majority of people choosing not to speak the truth about his obvious lack of covering. Whether inadvertent or willful, blindness only alters the experience of reality.

Consider the handicap of physical blindness. Those who live in darkness because their eyes fail to work properly, have real limitations. But only the *experience* of reality is altered, not what is truly real. The blind are unable to see the fullness of reality because their eyes do not effectively take in and interpret light impulses. Reality is the state of things as they *actually exist* as opposed to mere *perceptions.* Our personal perceptions may be lost in the shadows of darkness, or perhaps even tinged pink with a rose-colored lens. But reality is unchanged despite obscurity or impairment of the observer.

While it is commonly stated, "Perceptions are real," it would be better said that perceptions, or illusions, are real to the one who lacks true, or clear vision. *Clarity requires us becoming free from the captivity of our illusions*—which only comes through the Light of life. As Helen Keller, an inspirational woman who lost her sight as a small child is attributed as saying, "The only thing worse than being blind is having sight but no vision."

> *Clarity requires us becoming free from the captivity of our illusions*—which only comes through the Light of life.

You and I desperately need truth delivering new vision. In our own power, we only have impaired perceptions and spiritual blindness. Light was the antidote to the bondage of my confusion. Light restored order. Light revealed beauty. Light was the precursor of life, even as far back as in Genesis—and I hope you will see it's exactly the same for your life today.

Implications for Life

I desired real vision for my life in the midst of chaos and God gave it to me bit by bit as I walked by faith. But I had to answer tough questions and look into dark recesses of my soul as I purposed to let the light in. To explore the implications for your own life, here are some inquiries only you can answer.

- Do you honestly want order and clarity in your life story—even if it means giving up the comfortable captivity of your illusion?
- Are you really satisfied or do you feel a nagging void, an emptiness in going through the motions of life?
- Do you want to see anew—to have real vision into all you were designed to be, even if it involves acute pain in the quest for the long-term gain?
- Do you want to live with greater intention and purpose, leaving a lasting legacy for this life and for eternity?

If you answered, "Yes," I offer you four words to get started in your pursuit: *"Let there be light."* We must "let," or allow there to be light for our world to come into focus. But how, you may be asking? Jesus promised,

"…He that follows me shall not walk in darkness, but shall have the light of life." (John 8:12, *NKJV*)

The source of life who is also the Light of men, *lighting every person coming into this world* is Jesus. He is the Light that shined into darkness.[1] He is the Light that was and is rejected by many people because darkness is preferred as a cloak shrouding the reality of their deeds.[2]

So as an intentional and personal act, we must let there be Light…let it, allow it, permit it.

The choice to be freed from the illusion cloaked in darkness is one only you can make for yourself. It requires an active, affirmative decision, just as God actively moved, dispelling the void of darkness back in Genesis. You must invite His Spirit to actively move in your life to dispel the darkness and gain clarity. This may mean initiating a relationship with God through His son, Jesus, by calling upon Him to take away the burden of your sins. Or it may mean, if already a Christian, that you ask the Holy Spirit to shine a spotlight on anything that is separating you from an intimate relationship with Him.

Over the years chaos continued in the attempt to overwhelm and bind me. And in one form or another, for as long as we are alive on this earth the tactics of darkness will continue. As a young woman I resolved to live beyond the norm and fight against the destruction evil seeks to bring. But I had a hard lesson to learn that wasn't being taught at church: *resolve and personal zeal alone cannot win the battle.* Eventually heart wounds untended and unhealed will cause a beating heart to stop.

For more than twenty-four years with each cycle of gut-wrenching betrayal and the

> *Resolve and personal zeal alone cannot win the battle.*

pain of disillusionment, I fought the darkness seeking to engulf my heart. The chaos pummeled my mind. Doubt mocked the hope that I could ever be a trophy of God's grace. The voices of condemnation and fear scorned me as a fool to wait for a miracle. They reminded me I was alone as I sought to display Christ's forgiveness and His unconditional love for my former husband.

Time passed and I visited the gravesite of my first baby many times, remembering that oppressive day when I intensely became aware of the war against my soul. And then many years later this war closed in on multiple fronts. How could I ever be freed from the cycle of chaos and confusion? I felt as if I was being sifted like wheat. And just as Jesus had warned Peter of the enemy's desire to destroy his life, I knew Jesus was warning me. I was filled with an internal unease, a mixture of vulnerability and fear. Something dreadful that I couldn't see clearly loomed in the distance.

I prayed for understanding and strength, knowing the culmination of emotional and spiritual abuse my heart had sustained had worn me down. Tentacles of darkness clung to me, clawing with their talons, whispering their lies. I was so exhausted in this battle born alone. I asked my pastor, who knew some of what I endured in my marriage, to pray for me. He warned of how the enemy might attempt to get to me. An excerpt of my email response to him reveals my heart at that time:

> *I have no intention of failing at my mission and getting knocked out of the race I've run in faithfulness for so long. I recognize the vulnerabilities in me are accentuated to new levels of late. I know I am starved emotionally as a woman, and even Peter had purposed not to fail, but did. I am running with my eye on the prize and want to hear "well done." My mission is to be a trophy of grace, demonstrating in this life the superiority of Christ over Satan.*

But the cock would crow in my life as it had in Peter's. I would weep bitter tears of anguish just a few months later. How could I have succumbed to the lure of another man's admiration and adoration? My emotionally starved heart was drawn like a moth to a flame...and I was burned. The darkest thread of my tapestry was woven into the story of my life as I experienced the pain of betraying my Lord and Savior. I had purposed for so many years to not fail Him, raising the sword even as Peter zealously did on the night he betrayed Christ.

Yet, I learned that personal fortitude and strength are never a match for our relentless opponent. With tactics so subtle and seemingly harmless he finally snared my wounded heart. His enhanced ploys of deceit were customized, and they tripped me in the race I had vowed to run for God's glory.

Thankfully, just as during Peter's agony, the foundation for accessing the power of the resurrection was being laid. Beyond what I could have ever foreseen, the inconceivable occurred in this darkest of all my hours. In the midst of this new level of personal despair and sorrow, a new dimension came into focus—Freedom. By experiencing the truth of my own frailty and my utter desperation surrendered in the loving arms of Jesus Christ, I was liberated.

The prison doors of my heart were opened to let in the Light, but *only by reaching a state of absolute dependence and a deep realization of my utter inadequacy.* My march to complete spiritual liberty, restoration and enlightenment advanced toward abundance; it was the goal Jesus had for my life all along.

> By experiencing the truth of my own frailty and my utter desperation surrendered in the loving arms of Jesus Christ, I was liberated.

The Light began revealing fear-based thinking and relational strongholds of the enemy. Chinks in my self-made armor and the inborn nature of my complete insufficiency became apparent. Truth battled lies from the pit of darkness as the enemy continued his persistent assault, but this time to no avail. I was rescued to live with new purpose because *Jesus loved me in my time of greatest need, a time when I believed I deserved it least.* The stone was rolled away from the grave of my lifeless heart as I came to see:

Jesus' love for me never had anything to do with deserving it.

That's what makes it unconditional. There is no grading scale that determines how much love you and I are allowed. God's love for you and for me never has anything to do with our performance—good *or* bad. Ever.

And that my friend, is the entire foundation for grace.

Your Choice—See With Real Vision

I share all of this to encourage you. Wherever you are in life, no matter where you have been or what you have done, Jesus is ready to rescue you with His truth and give you real vision for living. Perhaps you're living in a place of apathy or despair. Or maybe you are one who's still under the illusion that trying harder and obeying the rules will merit more of God's favor. Whatever your situation, I implore you, please—*let there be Light.*

God is able, in unexplainable ways, to work all things together for our good and for His glory. He longs to free us from ourselves and the lies of the enemy so we can live the abundant life Jesus came to give.

"And you shall know the truth and the truth shall make you free." (John 8:32)

It is true. As the Light of the world promised, I was finally set free from the darkness lurking in deep recesses of my wounded and war-torn heart. I let Light penetrate the deepest places of my soul to expose my old illusions about who God is and who I am. The journey through a pathway of pain delivered greater vision as my aptitude for truth expanded. I wanted more Light and more Truth because He did not condemn me, He just loved me.

And even though the plot to my story was not to include the "happily ever-after" for my first marriage despite the years of begging, praying, crying and persevering, *I had come to a place where it was well with my soul.* I was at peace with the story line of my life despite acknowledging the fact that I still wish some things could have been different.

I know now, what I didn't know before: an overwhelming joy that supersedes the pain of deep sorrow. I've learned to experience intimacy with Jesus and know His deep abiding, unconditional love for me as I live in the power of grace and forgiveness. He, who loved me to death, is enough. This core truth set me free.

The Light abolishes the shadows of doubt and fear. I embrace the reality of my story folding into God's. A new dimension, ever-expanding in the universe of the soul emerges. Our Creator bestows light and revitalizes life through the power of His redemptive transformation.

He creates…He heals…He recreates…He restores.

Hopefully by now you see that God loves you enough to allow disillusionment in your life. He permits our brokenness and the brokenness of others to draw us to Him. He is awakening our core need for more Light. God allows painful circumstances into our stories for a greater purpose—to birth new vision within us. He loves and comforts us in the midst of grief while nurturing us to a place of even greater hope and deeper appreciation for His grace and His cause.

The Truth will dress your wounds and heal your broken heart if you offer them to Him. He will give you beauty for ashes during your quest for meaning and purpose—even as the battle continues to rage. Jesus longs for you to see the reality that *your world is falling into place as you fall into His everlasting arms.*

Shake off the chains that bind you and allow Jesus to remove the blinders preventing you from seeing clearly.

Are you ready?

Exceed the norm and choose life with real vision.

Let there be Light…to give you His perspective for your new life story.

KEYS TO THRIVE

See with Real Vision.

1) What has God allowed in your life story to shatter the illusion and bring you to a point of surrender to the truth and to greater enlightenment?
Divorce & Infidelity. Also - my son's battle

2) Do you intentionally "let" or allow the Light to shine into your heart regularly to prevent the daily effects of chaos in your life, or do you more typically seek it in response to an overwhelming crisis of chaos? *I intentionally seek it*

3) Do you understand how reactive Christian living is inferior to proactive living? *Yes!!.*

4) Describe how living in a reactive mode leaves your heart more vulnerable to the battle tactics of the enemy. *reactive mode means we are caught off*

5) Truth to ponder: John 8:12; Matthew 20:34; Mark 10:52; Luke 4:18

PART TWO

DISCERN YOURSELF WITH CLARITY

4

PERSPECTIVE IS EVERYTHING

Do You View Yourself with Broken Mirrors?

People are like stained-glass windows.
They sparkle and shine when the sun is out,
but when the darkness sets in,
their true beauty is revealed only if there is a light from within.

Elisabeth Kubler-Ross

"**M**irror, mirror on the wall—who is the fairest of them all?" These haughty words ring in our childhood memory as those spoken by the malevolent queen in the Grimm's tale of *Snow White and the Seven Dwarfs.* But have you ever stopped to consider that many times we utter lines from a similar script in our own stories?

It started when we were infants, born with a need for security. We asked rudimentary questions multiple times daily: "Will someone come to my help when I cry?" "Does my existence matter to anyone?" "Am I important?" The answers we received began to influence our perspective of self-worth.

Persistently and loudly we sought to have our basic needs fulfilled because literally, it was a matter of life and death. When we received acts of nurture and comfort, our brains were imprinted with messages of value and security, allowing for more complex emotional development and healthy self-awareness in the future. But for the child who was physically or emotionally neglected or abused, the uncertainty created anxiety. Fear-based thinking began to flourish. "Am I enough?" "Do I have what it takes?" Countless times these questions ring in the soul over a lifetime. The source we look to for answers will either put us into bondage or set us free.

> The source we look to for answers will either put us into bondage or set us free.

Perhaps as me, you can remember feelings of insecurity and inferiority nagging you as a child. One example I remember occurred back in elementary school. The Presidential Fitness Test was given yearly in gym class. Upper body strength was evaluated through the flexed-arm-hang for girls and pull-ups for boys. I always dreaded that day. Try as I might, my chin was never over that bar for more than two seconds.

It was painfully clear, I simply did not have what it took, and with the whole class looking on I failed time after time. While now, a seemingly insignificant event to an adult, these real inadequacies in a young life can be used by the enemy of our souls. He seeks to gain access to a child's heart because they are ill-equipped to combat the strategies of emotional assault, occurring both at home and at school.

Consequently for me, it was way back in the third grade that I began believing the lie that I was too fat, too ugly and somehow completely inferior to others. The flexed arm hang failures along with countless other incidents were used to firmly establish a broken mirror of self-reflection in my life.

You can imagine how this broken mirror spoke to me during my years of trying to improve my performance in an attempt to secure the love and affirmation I craved. "If you were just...prettier...smarter...like her...like him." "If you weren't so...stupid...ugly...fat...disappointing." "Can't you do better? What is wrong with you?" The imperfections in our life stories serve to confirm the lies, sinking the talons of an enemy deeper and deeper into our hearts as he seeks to define our perspective of who we are.

When we refer back to the wicked queen and her self-reflection, we see that she too is dealing with her own basic personal insecurities. She fully expects to be told that her beauty is superior. She is looking to have her value affirmed through the flawed metric of comparison with others. But when her expectations are defied, she experiences a crisis. As the rest of the story unfolds, her poor judgment driven by malignant self-interest, self-protection and pretense weave a plot between good and evil.

As unfortunate as it may be, we can see some parallels to real life. Poor decisions are frequently driven by our insecurity about who we are and serve as the underlying reason for many unhealthy and hurtful behaviors. Our natural tendency is to define our worth and identity by comparing ourselves to others. Thankfully, most people are not narcissistic sociopaths like the wicked queen. But an honest evaluation

> Fear and insecurity can lead us down paths of self-destruction.

of similarities is important because fear and insecurity can lead us down paths of self-destruction.

Some common themes are immediately obvious, while others are tragically insidious. In either case, the unfortunate truth is that who we are intended to be is often obscured by someone else. Our real and best self is chained up on the inside while our false-self manages life on the outside. When we manage inner fears and insecurity on our own we cannot discover our full potential as created. God designed us to connect to Him and become all that He purposed, but it requires intentionally getting real as we apply the truth.

Deep insecurities and the perceived need for self-protection have been part of our human nature ever since the fall of mankind back in the Garden. We tend to hide from the true mirror of truth, just like our first parents did. If we ever wish to become all we were intended as our real-self, the first step is to understand the fallen, sin-prone, false-self of our human nature. We will be able

> We will be able to rid ourselves of deceitful mirrors of self-reflection by deliberately choosing to see who we are in the light of the truth.

to rid ourselves of deceitful mirrors of self-reflection by deliberately choosing to see who we are in the light of the truth.

Sin Nature: A Reality Distorting Who You are in Christ

We'll begin by covering some stark facts that I'm hopeful will come as no shock. In your human state, you are a fallen being. I pray that you're also redeemed because you've reached out for God's great love manifested through the Light of the world. But as you may know, even though we're redeemed and forgiven through Christ, we are nevertheless still cursed by a sin-nature that may have far too much ongoing control over the course of our life story.

My inborn insecurities are taunted by fears, as are yours. I desire a security that is illusive. You and I yearn to feel safe and know we are valuable. We desire to know that we have what it takes. But, if left to ourselves, every human will seek answers from all the wrong places.

It is of critical importance to understand how the enemy of your soul strategically uses your own insecurities and questions about who you are to thwart the abundant life. If we can get honest with ourselves, we will be able to better anticipate how the enemy uses our own human nature against us.

Satan is seeking to ruin you and me; we have already covered this point in depth. And honestly, what better way to do so than to facilitate our own self-destruction? His cruelty is unending and he loves nothing more than for God's children to destroy themselves and waste their lives. He sneers at our ignorance as we fail to recognize the fact: we are frequently our own worst enemy.

Self: An Enemy We Need to Know

A statement made by Michael Corleone in *The Godfather Part II* is widely repeated and applicable to our subject at hand: "Keep your friends close but your enemies closer." Unfortunately, while difficult to admit, many times we are unwittingly our own worst foe. We fail to know ourselves when we refuse to investigate and acknowledge the uncomfortable truth about what is within us.

Just like Adam and Eve in the Garden, we may attempt to divert our accountability in the misguided effort to escape personal guilt and feelings of shame. After all, if we play the victim and blame our problems on someone else, we can maintain the inflated self-image we prefer. The human brain is well-equipped with the power to rationalize our behavior and create stories to explain away personal responsibility for flawed thinking, poor decisions and tragic outcomes. Our broken mirrors serve to reinforce what we want to believe while we remain under the spell of an illusion.

But I'm certainly not asserting that punishing ourselves mentally is the answer either. What I am advocating is that we strive for a healthy, balanced self-esteem which acknowledges the truth of our human state without beating ourselves up over being human. This balance grounded in truth allows us to embrace the origin of our real self-worth rather than pretending the basis of our value is dependent on our personal characteristics or performance.

Our goal is to see ourselves as God, our Creator, sees us. However, as we've noted previously, deliberately choosing truth over an illusion is not the most popular way to live. Much of society prefers living in a world of fantasy rather than taking a hard look at facts. Think about how many hours the average American mindlessly watches "reality" television while emotionally disconnecting from the reality of their own lives. For far too many, life is lived in detachment from self, God and others in an attempt to avoid the truth.

> For far too many, life is lived in detachment from self, God and others in an attempt to avoid the truth.

In this disconnected state we fail to know or understand the root issues that drive our thoughts, words and actions. It's natural to dislike pain and seek to avoid it. Thinking too deeply can stir up thoughts we'd rather not think about and feelings we'd prefer not to feel. Avoiding contemplation and introspection is the path of least resistance.

When seasons of crisis come, you may briefly entertain the question, "How did I get to this spot in my life?"

Unfortunately though, if the necessary time isn't taken, or if you honestly have never known how to explore the core questions of your soul, you may not have gotten truthful answers.

And therein lies the problem, and as you can see, the problem often lies within. We want to be esteemed the fairest, the brightest, and the best—not the broken, the flawed, and the weak. And so frequently it's easier to stick with the status quo and look at our reflection through broken mirrors of self-deceit. After all, projecting a false image to protect us from the reality of our fragile insecurities is what most people do, right?

The time to let go of these dysfunctional mirrors is now if we are serious about learning to thrive. Our identity and worth must become enlightened by Truth.

Truth One: The Broken Mirror of Comparison Always Distorts Reality

Let's begin with a look at a person who can teach us all something. It's a person who epitomizes the product of fallen Eve and is described in Proverbs chapter seven. This poor soul is easy to disdain. We can dismissively categorize her as someone completely unlike ourselves. After all, she works the streets downtown or near convention centers of our cities. She's a woman found in the red light districts of the world, far removed from our own world, right? Devoted to what's been touted as the world's oldest profession, she sells herself out to an act of corrupted intimacy, an act leading to death, not life.

When looking through the mirror of comparison, it is easy to see that you and I are definitely not like her, right?

But wait.

This woman is a descendent of Adam and Eve, just as we are. Maybe, just maybe there is something we should objectively examine about the sin-nature we *all* have within us. Depending on the version of Bible used, chapter seven of Proverbs describes this person as the "strange" woman, the "adulterous" woman or a "harlot." On the surface her likeness to us may be obscured by these descriptions in English. When we look at the Hebrew word used, however, it hits home. This word is actually a verb meaning, "to be strange or a stranger; to be estranged, be alienated, to be a foreigner, to be an enemy."[2]

We can all relate to this truth if we are honest. This person merely acts out *who they are at their core apart from God.* She is estranged, or alienated from her original purpose. Designed for something greater, she is separated from her Creator. She is His enemy due to her unredeemed nature. In acts now based out of her degraded condition and de-valued self-image, she prostitutes herself. She uses her life for an unworthy, corrupt purpose in an attempt to provide personal security and safety for herself apart from God.

Read the last paragraph again. Think about the content and be honest. Have you ever been guilty of using your life for a corrupted purpose based upon your own personal agenda? Have you

> She uses her life for an unworthy, corrupt purpose in an attempt to provide personal security and safety for herself apart from God.

ever attempted to create a sense of safety for your life apart from God? Do you ever seek to maintain a sense of control and create an environment to minimize vulnerability? How about maximizing your own personal pleasure at the expense of another; in other words, have you ever used people?

If honest, I believe we all have to regretfully answer, yes. Our mirror of comparison proclaiming us to be "the fairest" is deceitfully flawed.

Take a look at a sample of behaviors revealing the character of one estranged from God and His purpose.

- Seduces—uses flattery to deceive, gain credibility and trust
- Has a purposeful, hidden, personal agenda—subtle, sly of heart
- Is loud and impudent—brazen, immodest, a show-off
- Knows the language of religion—a chameleon
- Speaks manipulatively—acts like a familiar friend, appeals to pride and ego
- Calls attention to possessions—image conscious in the world's finery
- Skilled at creating diversions from reality—beautifies and perfumes the defiled bed, covering it with a temporary sweet smell to mask the stench of her actions
- Focused on comforting herself by alluring and using others—is a taker, gives only to meet her own agenda

When we are truthful and comparatively study of our own human nature, we see these characteristics may also reflect our thoughts, attitudes and actions—and yes, even among those of us who claim to be Christians. As Christians we are redeemed from the penalty of sin at the moment of salvation, but the power of sin within our human nature remains. We must actively and daily seek freedom from what lurks within our sin nature.

As we mature in Christ we learn to defy the power of sin by His strength. It is a process highly dependent on your personal desire for looking into the truth and your willingness to apply it. When acting out of our old nature, we demonstrate the same characteristic of the Proverbs seven woman: a person looking to survive, using all the normal human methods.

When sin continues to have power in the life of those claiming to be Christians, it's evidence that the enemy is prevailing in one way or another through the fallen human nature. Sadly, professing Christians may have life stories still full of death, not life, just like the person of Proverbs seven. Their speech may be drivel, rather than words of substance that nurture real health and healing. Their vision for life may remain willfully false if they're unwilling for the Light to confront dark corners of their hearts.

Many remain physically and emotionally driven rather than spirit driven. Their fleshly desires maintain the control despite their spiritual birth. They remain bound by shame and feelings of low worth. And in our fallen and fallible human nature, we all can cling to habitually dysfunctional behaviors based in self-protection and gratification. We hinder our own transformation when we fail to surrender to the protective truth of our Savior.

A transformed life is simply not possible utilizing the tools of the flesh and this world. When a person fails to look into the mirror of truth, unable or unwilling to be real with themselves, God and others, a life of self-preservation unfolds, just like for the wicked queen and the woman of Proverbs seven.

We like to be able to say, "Well at least I am not like them," while secretly pointing to someone making choices we believe we would never make. But this broken mirror of comparison is a barrier to authenticity. It perpetuates self-importance, self-reliance, self-centeredness, and self-righteousness, all of which are obstructions to intimacy with Christ.

If we're honest with ourselves, we know our need for security and affirmation can drive us to combat fear on our own terms, many times before we even realize it. Sometimes we look to the broken mirror of comparison as we seek to know who we are. But the wrong information about ourselves will simply lead us to another distorted looking glass: the broken mirror of control.

Truth Two: The Broken Mirror of Control Reflects Your False-Self

Not seeing ourselves as God sees us keeps us ruled by our perpetual human insecurities. Consequently, we cling to control in another misguided attempt to protect ourselves. But foolishly, just as Eve did, we exert our authority in matters beyond our scope, rather than submitting to the authority of God. The unanticipated outcome is living in the bondage of fear.

The person who struggles to be in control of every situation demonstrates that fear is ruling. The broken mirror of control

> Not seeing ourselves as God sees us keeps us ruled by our perpetual human insecurities.

proclaims falsely that we are safe because we are in charge. It confidently asserts we are secure and without vulnerability behind a wall of self-protection. But it sabotages the ability to authentically connect with God and others.

Because of each person's fallen state, fear torments all, regardless of gender. In our unspoken and many times unconscious desperation, we internally cry, "Mirror, mirror on the wall...Am I enough?" It is then that the mirror of control displays an image of the false-self. This is the part from which many people operate because of the perception of safety it offers. It reveals little of significance and minimizes vulnerability. It's a common barrier to the discovery of our authentic, real-self as intended by God.

Is Your False-Self in Charge?

Remember, people are uniquely designed by their Creator with different personalities and styles. You could read countless books on the ways human tendencies are categorized and the strengths and weaknesses of each. God desires us to glorify Him through the uniquely beautiful characteristics He created in each of us as individuals.

The false-self, however, is a perversion of who you and I were created to be. It's a product of sin and the flesh, not the rich beauty of who you and I are in our true-self, alive in God. Psychologists tell us it's developed as a protective mechanism beginning in childhood as a response to a chronic lack of empathy and abundance of shame. The more a child comes to feel that *who they are* is not appreciated or valued the more dominant the false-self becomes as a means of emotional survival.

The concept of the false-self within the study of psychology was first introduced by Dr. Donald Winnicott (1896–1971). As a pediatrician and psychoanalyst he explained that the false-self results in a poverty of inner life and a loss

> The false-self results in a poverty of inner life and a loss of innate vitality, joy and creativity.

of innate vitality, joy and creativity.[3] It is a persona of outward compliance or bravado suppressing vital parts of the real-self perceived to be unacceptable.

For example, when I felt humiliated and ashamed for being unable to perform the flexed arm hang successfully, I had to act out of my false-self to preserve my sense of public dignity and sense of value. "Oh well; I don't care!" These were words spoken but certainly not reflecting the truth of my heart. I did care. And I really wished I was more like little Cindy, who was a superstar, hanging there effortlessly for over two minutes every time the test came around.

But instead of authenticity, the false-self ruled. I was unable at the time of my disappointment to appropriately comfort myself with the truth while acknowledging the reality of my sadness. The truth was that my value did not diminish due to lack of upper body strength; however, in that moment when battling the condemning internal voice of shame, I used pretense (deceit) rather than truth as my weapon because it was all I knew to do.

Are you starting to see how insidious the development of the false-self can be? Whether shielding us from the shame we may feel with minor emotional traumas, or from the blows delivered by egregious physical, sexual or emotional abuse, the false-self helps us regulate internal pain. What examples can you remember from your childhood when feelings of shame were managed by your false-self? The frequency, intensity and source of your experience with shame will determine how dominant your false-self is today and how your enemy uses it to keep you from authentic relationship with yourself, God and others.

My false-self, likely as yours, became even more entrenched when growing older. Teenage years taught us how to protect ourselves emotionally with more pretending. We participated in the "one-up, one-down" game, putting down others in an unconscious effort to feel better about ourselves. Girls were ruthless with cutting words. The comparisons among others persisted and controlling the situation meant controlling one's image.

Growing up as a church kid regretfully did not help. The same comparison games were played there too, just with pious flair. I learned to protect myself from exposure to ridicule and judgment just like many others have. A culture of image management prevailed. Weaknesses were not to be revealed and impostors were unwittingly groomed. Sin was hidden. Desperate marital situations were not revealed. Deep wounds of the heart were not acknowledged and healed. Smiles were affixed. The situation was controlled. Embarrassment to the family was averted.

And sadly, the cycle continues in many lives and in many churches.

The protective facade has many faces. It's lived on a continuum of mostly unrecognized inner desperation, applying to people with and without faith. Take a look at our sad attempts to keep ourselves emotionally safe by reviewing behaviors summarized on the following table.

One end of the behavior continuum is labeled aggressive or domineering and the other is labeled passive or daunted. You'll likely find your chosen style for maintaining personal safety and control with some overlapping characteristics. However, we usually fall toward one pole of the spectrum or the other.

Faces of Control
The False-Self Lived On the Continuum of Desperation

Aggressive/Domineering	Passive/Daunted
Motto: "If I take charge I will be safe"	Motto: "If I can get you to take care of me I will be safe"
Aggressively demands control	The passive "wallflower;" does not want to be in charge
Powerful & leverages power (manipulates) to get his or her way; overtly pushy	Weak willed; gives in to other's demands; or may covertly be manipulative in a "nice" way
A bully; verbally unkind & loud when things do not go his or her way; pouts & punishes	A people pleaser; cannot say no; lacks healthy interpersonal boundaries; the quiet martyr; likely to be passive-aggressive
Superficial in relationships; Thinks & speaks for others close to him or her; "I know best" attitude without seeking to know the desires of the other person	Superficial in relationships; Allows others to make the decisions because if others are "happy" it is safe; reveals no real personal desires or strong opinions; avoids all conflict
Vulnerability is viewed as a danger: afraid to let others & God in; "takes care" of self	Vulnerability is viewed as a danger: must have someone else "taking care" of him or her
"Love" is not unconditional; Does for others to leverage or maintain control	"Love" is not unconditional; Does for others to receive something (care, attention, accolades, a sense of value, etc...)
No peace, no rest, no joy; busy being "large and in charge"	No peace, no rest, no joy; living out of duty, not desire
Does not trust God: I can manage it all myself; He has made me more capable than others	Does not trust God: I am a distinguished victim in need of others to care for my needs

Keep in mind that the importance of knowing our fallen nature is to better foresee how the enemy may attempt to use it against us. Don't let the enemy use the truth of what you discover to shame you into hiding. An honest self-evaluation of how our sinful condition operates is a first step in preparing for strategic combat. Please don't let our adversary distract you from introspection. And don't allow him to deject you as you become enlightened to the unfavorable truth about your own false-self. As individuals, we must understand more clearly why we are prone to do what we do. Only then can we effectively deactivate dysfunctional triggers.

As an adult with a false-self largely in control, perhaps you've told the diversionary lie to yourself and others for so long it's become believable: "It doesn't matter…forget it…I don't care anymore."

But the truth is that it does matter.

You matter.

And it's time to give your insecurities and old wounds to God for healing. We will explore this further in our next chapter. But the first step is to refuse the false reflection that seems to protect you from the reality of pain from within.

Decide to thrive and abandon the impostor.

Your choice will begin a journey of becoming.

Becoming the real you.

KEYS TO THRIVE

Abandon Your False-Self.

1) Do you have any trouble with the thought that you are made of the same stuff as the worst sinner you can imagine? (Consider Romans 3:23) *No*

2) Had you ever realized your need for control (demonstrated through living as your false-self) to be a symptom of fear and the need for safety? *yes — when my Dad left & my Mom fell apart ... began the need to control ....*

3) Where on the continuum of the false-self do you fall? Aggressive and domineering or passive and daunted?

4) What has God revealed to you about your own broken mirrors of self-reflection? Do you see yourself as a new creation in Christ? *I mostly see myself as new creation — wrote on FB about it*

5) Truth to ponder: 2 Corinthians 5:17; Ephesians 4:22-24; 2 Corinthians 10:12

5

THE POWER OF SIN'S BITE

Are You One of the Walking Wounded?

The sting of death is sin...
But thanks be to God, who gives us the victory through
our Lord Jesus Christ.

1 Corinthians 15:56 & 57

O n the journey of becoming our best self, most of us have either fallen or gotten pushed down more than once. We live in a sinful world so there is no escaping getting hurt one way or another. But we are survivors. God has created the human brain with an amazing capacity to isolate unspeakable circumstances and events so that we can endure the associated pain in that moment.

What's past is indeed, past. The goal of looking back is never to dwell unnecessarily on the pain of old memories. The goal we have now, however, is to assess the state of our current emotional and spiritual health. An assessment of true healing is required to ensure that our hearts have the capacity to thrive in full vitality and intimacy with Christ. We must in cooperation with God's Spirit, assess any heart wounds. We must allow Him to pull back the old bandages and show us what may have been hidden.

Because everyone on the face of this planet has been injured in one way or another, our brokenness is the great equalizer among us. Some wounds are simply byproducts of the fall and those tied to original sin. We arrived in the delivery room broken, exposed to the sting of sin within us even before our first breath. These are the wounds common to all; let's call them exposure wounds. Exposure wounds relate back to the fact that God's glory no longer clothes mankind. We are exposed and naked before Him in our spiritually dead state. Something originally intended is missing and our hearts hurt with a longing for it.

Each child enters the world with vulnerability embedded in their unredeemed heart: it's the fear of inadequacy. And as self-awareness develops, we become aware of feeling general shame and the fear of becoming exposed. Consequently, a child is highly susceptible to core shaming by parents or others, which leads to the development of the false-self as we learned in the last chapter.

As a child grows to believe he or she is inadequate and inferior, self-hatred and a perspective of low self-worth may become embedded within the heart and mind. Whether intentional or not, unhealthy parenting and the lack of emotional and spiritual nurture are often used by the enemy during childhood years. Destructive, fear-based thought patterns are initiated and dysfunctional coping mechanisms are adopted as a matter of emotional self-defense against exposure wounds.

Then there is more. Additional trauma adds to our injuries through either our own

> Lack of emotional and spiritual nurture are often used by the enemy during childhood years.

disobedience, or someone else's sinful words and actions directed toward us. These are the inflicted wounds.

Just as falling down physically breaks the skin open to rupture what once was intact, hearts can be broken in like manner. If not appropriately treated, a physical wound is susceptible to opportunistic disease and infection, which always extends the tissue damage. Our hearts are vulnerable to opportunistic disease as well. A wounded heart must be properly cared for to optimally heal. Our response to wounding events becomes a critical factor for our soul's health.

The wound must be cleaned and bandaged, or "bound up" as beautifully described in Isaiah 61:1. The passage is quoted again by Jesus in Luke 4:18 as He initiated His earthly ministry. He proclaimed His purpose to a wounded, diseased, and sin-stained world:

> *"...the LORD...has sent me to bind up the broken-hearted, to preach deliverance to the captives, to recover sight to the blind, to set at liberty them that are bruised."*

God knew we were broken and captive to our own blindness. Sadly, a festering injury left unchecked and unhealed will only get worse even if hidden by Band-Aids or declared unimportant. Ugly symptoms of the infection will corrupt our lives and then spread to the lives of those around us if we don't give the wound and our subsequent emotions to Him. A common saying with which you may be familiar is quoted something like this: "wounded people wound people." And it is true.

Wounded parents damage their precious children. Wounded husbands hurt their wives. Wounded wives injure their husbands. The cycle goes on and on. Without the healing balm of the Great Physician a wound ignored will forever be a wound unhealed, tainting individual lives, perhaps for generations.

Dr. Winnicott shares his medical and psychological expertise by observing: "The world is full of the walking wounded: people of outward success and respectability who are not quite real on the inside, who inflict their wounds on others."[1]

Not quite real on the inside...

But is that a problem, you may ask?

You could read countless books written about the psychological effects of trauma. You could take classes and attend seminars. You could spend thousands of dollars in a psychologist's or counselor's office. I have done all of these to learn about how we as living souls are affected mentally, emotionally and spiritually by the traumas we sustain in this broken world.

Yes, being not quite real is a problem.

We need to systematically assess and treat the root issues to experience the freedom found only with inner healing of our souls. Think about this to understand the complexity: we are spiritual beings having a physical experience in this life. Your spirit is having a physical experience while housed in your physical body. Our thoughts and emotions, the expressions of our heart or soul, are physical, chemical changes occurring within the physical structure of our brain. Medical science validates that traumatic events and subsequent negative thought patterns cause brain chemistry to be altered. Dysfunctional coping mechanisms become neurologically imprinted pathways in our brains.

Consequently, an effective treatment plan for heart wounds must involve recognition of the impact they've had on our entire triune being: body, soul and spirit. All successful care plans for physical, emotional or spiritual health issues begin the same way: Take the first step to healing with one intentional choice—*acknowledge.*

Care Plan for Healing: Step One—Acknowledge the Wound

If you want true healing and a renewed heart and mind, the first step is to acknowledge the problem. The injury happened—it existed or exists. Acknowledging is not blaming, nor is it excusing bad behavior or sin. Acknowledging is to realize the fact of your brokenness and to admit that you want to do something about it. This would seem to be simple, but for most people, it's not easy to do. You see, acknowledging a wound usually involves going back to some darker days. It brings up emotions ranging from disappointment to terror. It involves examining deep recesses of your heart long-ago walled off from yourself, others, and even withheld from God. This requires more than a simple exercise of the conscious intellect. Rather, it involves deep and often unconscious matters of the heart.

> If you want true healing and a renewed heart and mind, the first step is to acknowledge the problem.

Our first wounds commonly occur somewhere in childhood. The enemy of our soul starts early in his strategy to destroy us, and many times he will first use the wounded adults in our lives to begin the process. Despite best intentions, no perfect parent exists. Like us, they were on their own journey with their own set of issues. Most were doing the best they could with what they knew. We can empathize and forgive more easily when we humanize those who have hurt us. But in some cases, parents are overwhelmed with strongholds of darkness of an ever greater degree. These are the parents who purposefully inflict wounds upon their children in despicable and malicious ways. Without natural affection, their depravity inflicts unfathomable and complex wounds that sear deeply.

I do pray this level of wounding isn't part of your story. But if it is, please know you are beloved by God. Allow His truth to heal you and set you free. You are precious. Large or small, your wounds matter to Him because they represent the sin that nailed Jesus to the cross. The injuries your heart and mind sustained not only caused deep sorrow to you, but also to Him. He is faithful, and His grace and love can and will heal your heart despite the scars you will continue to bear in this life.

Perhaps your heart wounds were inflicted by repetitively piercing words and actions, or by general emotional neglect and lack of interaction. Your heart may be imprisoned by the shame and condemnation inflicted upon you by adults who may or may not have intended to hurt you. Maybe you don't love yourself as you've been created. You feel secretly flawed and inferior. Perhaps you believe you are not enough—or that you are just too much. Whatever the case, you're hiding at some level.

It may very well be that you are one of the "normal" walking wounded. A fairly "functional" false-self may rule as a matter of your status quo. You may believe that you are "fine" despite some baggage. But here is the truth: no matter if intended or unintended, large or small, seemingly trivial or heinous, wounds and their effects are a part the human experience. That includes our parents, you and me, and our children. And these emotional injuries sustained but untreated will affect our personal understanding of some foundational life issues.

The issues of our identity and purpose.

It's crucial for us to now understand that the way we were taught to answer the questions, "Who am I?" and "Does my life matter?" shapes the direction of our lives. During our critical formative years, our parents and authority figures were positioned to influence us our perspective about ourselves. Sometimes part of the acknowledgment necessary for healing will involve the need for remapping beliefs about the answers we received to these questions. If we prayerfully seek guidance from God, His Spirit will guide into the truth we individually need. Begin asking Him to reveal any lies you may have grown up believing about yourself.

Potential Father Wounds

Fathers have a special position in a child's life. They endow a child's physical identity and paternal name as his descendent. But he also impacts identity on a much deeper level. A father is to represent the nature and character of God to his children, showcasing the strength and power of our Heavenly Father who selflessly provides and protects.

Psychologically and emotionally a father has the power to bestow a healthy identity. He may also create a deep core of shame within the child by verbally or non-verbally communicating that he won't *identify with them* because they aren't good enough for him. Emotionally healthy fathers are able to bestow a healthy sense of identity by expressing consistently positive words verified through non-disparate actions. His life reiterates over time that his children are loved and important to him, not because of what they do or don't do, but merely *because of who they are as his child.*

When a father displays delight in his child for who they are, he creates an environment of safety. In this security the child has the freedom to be authentically themselves. By protecting them physically, emotionally and spiritually, he helps them discover who they really are created to be. He empathizes. He sees their world through their eyes at all developmental stages and serves as their advocate.

When he celebrates his child's gifts and admires their unique individuality as distinctly separate from himself, he nurtures real growth of their real selves. A father facilitates a healthy and God-centered perception of identity in his child by focusing on learning who he personally is in Christ. It's only by understanding his own identity that he's able to then humbly execute his God-given responsibility for the souls of his children.

Secure children come from emotionally healthy families. These are led by parents who are personally secure because as adults they understand who they are as God's child. A child's security is imparted in the same way. Sons and daughters come to know who they are because of "whose" they are. This foundational sense of belonging is crucial for ongoing emotional development and healthy self-awareness. Regrettably however, not all fathers are emotionally strong and spiritually mature in the leadership of their children, thus the cycles of dysfunction repeat.

> Sons and daughters come to know who they are because of "whose" they are.

Many dads wound their children inadvertently because they haven't dealt with their own shame, core insecurities, unforgiveness and anger. Wounds of abandonment and rejection can be inflicted not only through physical abuse by a father, but also through emotional abuse. Children who are shamed and devalued by toxic words, frequent yelling, and hurtful behaviors of commission and omission end up with wounds similar to the physically abused child.

A child's ongoing and seemingly futile effort to win the approval of a father delivers a painful message and leads to a child's self-contempt and anger. With or without words these children are told: "There is something bad about you...you aren't good enough...you can never get things right..." Shame and anger experienced over the years often leads to self-hatred and a multitude of behavioral and emotional issues. The root issues at the heart of that which will bind them stem from the child's reactions to the physical or emotional rejection they're forced to endure. Shame for who they *are* become binding chains.

When father wounds are inflicted and remain unhealed by God, adolescents move into adulthood without ever experiencing freedom. They're unable to joyfully embrace and develop the innate creativity and vitality that comes from the security of knowing who they really are. Teens learn to compensate and survive, but the beauty of their true individuality will be tainted by the deceit of their false-selves.

Does this apply to you? You may appear well-equipped to emotionally protect yourself, confidently asserting you can cope with whatever life throws your way. But a false-self developed to meet the demands of a father's dysfunction only masks the core wound. Even if your father's unhealthy behavior patterns were inadvertent, self-protective, compensatory measures may have become well-developed to help you survive for a season. But they prevent the healing and true freedom we crave.

Potential Mother Wounds

A mother has a closely related, but different role as parent. She represents the beauty, nurture and loving care of God to her children. From the moment of conception she is the child's earliest life sustaining force. As she meets the child's emotional and physical needs, she is answering deeply embedded questions pertaining to worth. The way we were loved and nurtured by our mothers teaches us what to believe about our value.

If you were sacrificially loved and cared for, you were reassured of your worth. She proved that you were valuable to her. But if this isn't what you primarily experienced, injury occurred. A mother who belittles or fails to empathize with her children inflicts wounds calling into question a child's sense of self-worth. "Am I really valuable? Does my life matter?" Without a mother who consistently demonstrates positive reassurance to these questions, the sad conclusion fostered by the enemy of the child's soul is, "No; you are worthless."

A distant mother or one unable to be pleased is one who has her own inner wounds and unmet needs. She will inadvertently, or in some sad cases purposefully inflict the injury of rejection. She passes her own wounded sense of personal value to her children because she is in her own bondage and in need of healing. But wounds may also be passed on in a more subtle manner. A mother who is clingy and uses her children to meet her own emotional or physical needs sends a similar message. "Your developmental needs aren't as important as mine. You aren't as valuable as me. You're an object...an accessory, and you're here to make me happy."

Does any of this have a familiar ring? Is God's Spirit causing you to feel unsettled as deep issues related to your mom are stirred within you? I understand; you may have become very stoic and efficient, having learned to perform well in the effort to win love and parental esteem. Or you may have given up at some point and learned to underperform or act out in negative ways for attention. Either way, you just wanted to know you were worthy to be seen and heard as an individual.

The temptation may be to say, "Oh, just forget it." After all, the past is the past and it's easier to keep it buried and out of mind. You appreciate your parents doing the best they could and don't want to seem ungrateful, unkind, or dishonor them. Or perhaps, your childhood was truly awful but you've packaged it neatly, preferring never to think about those painful experiences again.

I get it. None of us like pain, even if it is only acute and temporary. But no matter your upbringing, I encourage you to prayerfully sit with the Lord and do a wound check. It's a critical first step on your path to real freedom. Ask Him if there is anything hidden within your heart that you need to acknowledge. Sit and wait. Listen. Journal your thoughts. Take a peek under any old bandages to make sure nothing is festering within you unaware.

Allow the healing to begin

> ✳ As you begin to prayerfully explore the deeper parts of your heart, refer to the free tools and resources available at kayemcarter.com/setfreetothrive/resources.

Care Plan for Healing: Step Two—Identify Lies Related to Wounds

The original injuries in and of themselves seem like enough to deal with, but your reactions to them are really the issue we need to shine the light upon. What we do or don't do at the time we are hurt will allow or prevent captivity by the enemy. This is a crucial concept to understand if you desire complete freedom. What we do with a wound's festering drainage can result in more damage if left untreated. Deeper harm, with the power to spiritually bind you for a lifetime, often occurs when we fail to deal with a wound appropriately. Just like a bleeding swimmer will attract sharks, a wounded heart will draw the attention of spirtual sharks. They recognize the opportune time to strike is while we are hemorrhaging.

Remember the context of war we live in? Various messengers within the kingdom of darkness skillfully extend the damage of early foundational traumas. Perhaps the original wounding came through careless words; possibly a parent putting you down or comparing you to another sibling in an unfavorable manner. It could have been an influential person humiliating and shaming you, telling you consistently through words and actions that you and your efforts were not good enough. You began to believe you were worthless as created, thus you had to perform to earn love.

Or perhaps the wound was inflicted through traumatic loss, such as a close family member's death or act of abandonment. Maybe your innocence was stolen by one you should have been able to trust. It could have been as simple as repetitive experiences of little personal failures (like my flexed arm hang experience) and hurtful words by peers. Your inexperience and youth likely prevented your ability to apply truth for the healing and protection of your heart.

Regardless of mode, fear and doubt are agents of the father of lies. They stand ready to pounce upon the wounded heart with their diabolical and deceitful whispering. "You are a nobody...No one cares about you... You are worthless...No one really loves you...No one even likes you...You are stupid...ugly...scrawny...fat... weird...different...You simply aren't good enough and never will be." The derogatory accusations come with a variety of barbs, do they not? They're masterfully employed to destroy your concept of who you really are and the innate value of being you.

While you may have heard that this is merely the negative self-talk that can be cured by the power of positive thinking, the truth is that it's really a much deeper issue. Although they may be helpful, the Band-aids of self-affirmation cannot heal your heart and free you from the power of the enemy's lies. Pervasive mental accusations represent the work of the deceiver. He seeks to have you enter into an agreement, or a spiritual contract with him. In fact, it's likely that your negative thoughts are an indication that you've already entered into a binding

> Although they may be helpful, the Band-aids of self-affirmation cannot heal your heart and free you from the power of the enemy's lies.

agreement. You see, if he can trick you into agreeing with his terms, in other words, his lies—*he will gain a foothold into the core of who you are. He will have binding dominion of at least a piece of your heart.*

What?

Please allow me to explain.

Any agreement between two parties is called a covenant, a vow, or a contract. And while you may never have considered this from within a spiritual context, we must. Understanding this concept will revolutionize your Christian walk. When we agree with any lie from the enemy, we enter into agreement with him. It doesn't matter if we did so inadvertently. To believe Satan's deceit is to believe that which is in opposition to the truth.

Not only does his deceit cripple you spiritually, but it becomes a powerful force controlling the way you think and make decisions. Literally, your brain's chemistry is changed as the lies map neurologic pathways internally.

His deceit actually becomes physically embedded within your thought patterns and your spiritual problem becomes chemically reinforced.

How many times have you and other Christians you've known continued year after year to struggle with persistent sinful thought patterns and oppressive addictive behaviors? Why is it that despite willpower, tears and prayer they cannot be shaken? If the truth of the gospel has set us free, then how is it that we still live as captives, seemingly powerless to get out of these prisons? The answer lies in the agreements we've made with our enemy.

> Not only does Satan's deceit cripple you spiritually, but it becomes a powerful force controlling the way you think and make decisions.

How can people who claim to be Christians with so much potential in Christ continue to destroy their lives and those of their families? *It is because of their long-standing agreements with the prince of the power of the air.* The lack of victory is due to spiritual contracts initiated when we believed his lies, many times traceable to a vulnerable time of wounding in our past.

Remember, when Adam sinned Satan gained spiritual dominion in this world.[2] He currently holds a position of spiritual authority, but for a limited amount of time. He counts on all humans, including Christians, to be ignorant of the spiritual hierarchy he rules. And because of this lack of awareness, he easily maintains his own coercive agenda and expands his kingdom.

Satan's purpose to thwart the power of God's plan in our life is accomplished when he takes our heart captive. *This occurs when we believe him rather than the Truth.* We cannot break spiritual strongholds or contracts with the enemy, in our own human power. Christians who struggle with negative thought patterns or addictive behaviors demonstrate the evidence of unbroken and binding agreements with the prince of the power of the air. These contracts cannot be broken by willpower or positive thinking. Many people are snared, unaware of the seriousness of their inner dialogue. Whether a Christian or not, our inner healing and freedom is prevented by believing Satan's answers to core questions about our identity or value.[3]

Satan hates each of us and would love to damn each soul to Hell. But once our spirits are made alive by personally trusting Jesus Christ as our Lord and Savior, he knows that he cannot separate us from God. And so he settles for nullifying our impact in the kingdom of God. He's happy to steal what could have been our eternal reward by limiting the impact our life has for the cause of Christ.

The enemy is quite satisfied watching you and me merely go through the motions of a Christian life. He laughs as we miss out on all we could have been. He takes pleasure in lives wasted because of failure to believe the Truth and then love God with *all* of our heart, soul and mind. He knows the important details of what you haven't acknowledged yet: *you don't have access and control over all of your heart because you gave away little pieces to him when you vowed allegiance to his lies.*

> The enemy is quite satisfied watching you and me merely go through the motions of a Christian life.

Although he cannot have all of you, and he can't have your *spirit* once you've given it to Jesus Christ, Satan is satisfied with the access he continues to have to your *heart*. With control of your heart he understands that he can control your thought patterns and emotions. Satan has all the leverage needed to inhibit complete intimacy with God when you allow him to have even a little piece of your heart.

Pause for a moment; read that again slowly.

This is deep, but life altering stuff. We cannot obey what Jesus asserted was the first and greatest commandment, which is to love the Lord God with **all** of our heart, if any part of our heart is not submitted to Truth. If even a small part of my heart remains inaccessible because it's controlled by the lies of the enemy then I am in disobedience, inadvertent as it may be.

> Satan has all the leverage needed to inhibit complete intimacy with God when you allow him to have even a little piece of your heart.

Oh, how I wish I'd been taught about these enemy tactics back in my childhood and in my adolescence and young adulthood. So much might have been altered for me had I understood the inner world of my thoughts. When I finally understood that *believing the enemy's lie about my value and who I am is a matter of my personal sin,* everything about "normal" Christian life changed. I found real freedom from broken mirrors of comparison and control once I identified the specific lies with which I had been duped for so many years. When I repented of my sin of agreeing with the enemy, rather than agreeing with the truth, I experienced victory through the power of Christ. Intimacy in our relationship became possible because He had access to all of my heart.

Care Plan for Healing: Step Three—Break Your Agreements with the Father of Lies

Offering our wounded hearts to anyone or anything but God and His truth sets us up for addictive bondage, in one form or another. Addictions are the "medication" one uses in the attempt to reduce the pain of an unhealed wound. They are merely symptoms of a deeper root issue.

Treating addictions with various forms of talk-therapy, behavior-modification and support groups can offer some palliative benefit and *help*, but cannot *heal* the original injury and deal with the root sin.

Our wounded, broken hearts must be intentionally given to our Redeemer who came to rescue us from bondage. This rescue wasn't only from the bondage of the *penalty* of sin for eternity, but also from the *power* of sin in our lives. For this to occur we must enter into full agreement with the Truth. We are set apart for God's glory and purpose at the moment we accept Him into our lives by faith. The derivative growth and maturity is a process. God desires to show us the barriers still remaining alive in our human nature that prevent us from being freed from the power of sin. These barriers will always be centered in what we really believe…that is, in whom we really trust.

Acknowledge that Your Wounded Heart Matters

To break an agreement with the father of lies, you must enter into a new agreement—an agreement with the Truth. This means you agree with Jesus that your injury or wound mattered. Name it and give it specifically to the Lord and ask for healing. It mattered to Christ because the sin that wounded you is sin that nailed Him to the cross.

You are beloved and He has been waiting for this moment in time when you fully and consciously give him your whole heart, including those broken pieces you've been trying to hide. He wants to heal those broken memories and negative emotions, binding them up in the power of His redemptive and transformative love. He desires you to experience the wholeness you have in Him.[4]

But for this to occur you must *desire real healing*, not another fancy Band-aid. Submitting to the treatment plan of the Great Physician means you surrender to His prescriptive plan for intentionally breaking the covenants you've made with the enemy. You must trust Him and His truth and turn away from lies and the old thought patterns that have become so familiar, they are like a part of you.

Confess Your Sin & Renounce the Liar's Power Through the Truth's Victory

The most important component of annulling agreements with the father of lies is to *humbly confess our own sin*. This is *not* to be confused with the sin of the original inflicted wound. Whoever hurt you and me will be held accountable by God for their misdeeds. You are never the cause of another person's sin; don't let the enemy shame you into believing that you somehow deserved it. Someone else's sin against you and against God is for them to confess. They may or may not repent, but don't allow your healing to be thwarted by focusing on them. God is the judge and tells us they will pay the eventual consequence if they remain unrepentant.[5] But you and I must confess the *lies we came to believe because of the wound.*

You are responsible only for your response. The sin that must be recognized and confessed is that of *believing the lie that came as a result of the wounding.* For example, perhaps like me, you must repent of believing that you are worthless unless perfect…you aren't good enough…you aren't lovable as you are…you are inferior…shameful…an embarrassment. This step of repentance in your treatment plan cannot be omitted, and it's the step for which trying harder, support groups and all the willpower in the world cannot effectively substitute.

In addition, you may need to confess any anger, unforgiveness, or bitterness you may have harbored against someone who's hurt you. Forgiving those who have wounded us frees us from the bondage in which we are doomed to live, should we choose to hold a grudge. But if we are honest, we have no forgiveness to offer in our own human strength.

It is not within our human nature to forgive a person in whom we should have been able to trust. It's only a supernatural forgiveness, through the power of Christ, that a person can forgive someone for stealing their innocence or betraying them. Being used or being taken for granted over time leads to feelings of rage and hatred, feelings that can consume and take root in bitterness if not dealt with head on. A child physically, sexually or emotionally abused will feel these negative emotions and likely not know what to do with them. Any time we feel our inherent value rejected through someone's actions and words, a deep anger is incited at an injustice we may or may not fully understand.

But when we are honest with God about our feelings, and we tell Him we are choosing to forgive as an act of obedience because of our desire to fully surrender to Him— He gives us His divine power to do so. It's through our authentic interaction with God, in dependence solely in the power of Christ, that we are freed from the chains binding us to old hurts. Only then are we released from the power of those negative emotions. I've told Him in anguish many times over the years, "Lord, I have no forgiveness to offer…please give me yours to give to them."

Ask Jesus to reveal to you all of the lies you have believed about yourself and then humbly repent of each of them. Ask Him to reveal any areas of unforgiveness or bitterness toward others. The Holy Spirit is your counselor desiring to lead you into all truth.

"However, when He, the Spirit of truth has come, He will guide you into all truth." (John 16:13a, *NKJV*)

Through the power of Jesus Christ's sacrifice on the cross, the keys to death and hell were won. In the name of Jesus and because of His spilled blood, the enemy and his minions have *no hold over you except that which you allow.* As you specifically repent for the lies you've believed and for any harbored unforgiveness, renounce the power of Satan and his messengers in your life by claiming the truth. The truth is that Jesus won your victory through His sacrificial work on the cross. His resurrection conquered the power of death. Claim all He has delivered to you as his beloved child and thrive in it.

By making the choice to be healed, you will be set free. Press into Jesus and come out of the captivity that's based entirely in deception by the enemy. Jesus came to heal all of your wounds and the subsequent damage caused by the lies. Your potential has been sabotaged through the confusion for far too long. But you will have to make a choice: the decision to follow God's care plan for your soul.

Defy the chaos in your life that's perpetuated by living as one of the walking wounded.

Exceed beyond the norm…be healed.

You will find that allowing Jesus access to all of your heart leads to a life of real vitality—the abundant life.

KEYS TO THRIVE

Be Healed.

1) Take time to get alone with God and prayerfully ask Him to reveal truth. Meditate on Psalm 51:6.

2) What lies of the enemy have you believed about yourself and about God as a result of wounds from your past? Make a list.

3) Believing a lie is sin because it opposes God's truth about what He declares about you and Himself. Take time to repent specifically for each lie God reveals to you. Then renounce the power of Satan to control you. Break all agreements you've made with him by claiming the power of Jesus' victory over sin and death in your life.

4) Begin to meditate on your story of redemption—an exciting chapter occurring even now through your heart's healing and deliverance.

5) Truth to ponder: Luke 4:18, Romans 5:1-2; 1 Peter 2:9, Philippians 1:6; 2 Corinthians 4:1-7

Jesus came to proclaim LIBERTY for the captives + recovering of sight to the blind, to set free those who are oppressed + to proclaim the year of the Lord's favor!

6

BEHOLDING YOUR IDENTITY

Do You Know Who You Really Are?

Behold, you desire truth in the inward parts:
And in the hidden part you will make me to know wisdom.

Psalm 51:6, NKJV

Despite technology and unlimited access to more information than one could ever hope to consume, we still wrestle with core questions about our identity, as did the ancients. You and I are not the first to begin this inner journey of contemplation as we take our question to God. Those who recognize their own awakening all began with this same question, *"Who am I?"* The most difficult part of obtaining answers can be in staying with the question long enough. The other difficulty is in abandoning the false illusion to which we may have become accustomed. To know ourselves fully and authentically we must be committed to a process, desiring wholly to see ourselves as our Creator sees us, recognizing His desire to make us to know wisdom.

Let's explore this process of enlightenment and the impact of learning to behold ourselves in the mirror of God's glory and holiness. We will begin by looking at one person's life story from long ago, the life of Moses. He is known to many people, even those without faith, thanks to Charlton Heston and years of reruns broadcasting the 1956 drama, *The Ten Commandments*. Moses was the influential and divinely inspired leader chosen by God to bring the Israelites out of captivity to Egypt. But his story also included an awakening and release from his own bondage.

Identity Revealed In a Desert Concealed

As we examine the back-story of Moses, we find we actually have a lot in common with him. He was a child born to common parents in a time and place where life was hard. The power of evil and godless governmental leadership was oppressive. But God's plan was unstoppable. Moses' story was to be written into His. Miraculously preserved after birth by the grace of God, Moses was raised in enemy territory and positioned for an unanticipated future. When we pick up his story in Exodus chapter two, he's in a season of preparation for an unplanned adventure.

The setting takes us to the backside of a desert in Africa after he'd fled Egypt for his life. In a fit of vengeance and unbridled passion, Moses had committed murder; then he ran. One might think the adopted grandson of the Pharaoh would have had other options, but Moses took the circumstances further into his own hands and decided to just disappear.

Driven by guilt and shame, he ended up in a place of isolation—*a place created by himself in the attempt to control his story and shroud his identity.* It's the consistent destination of the fleshly false-self that always seeks self-protection. In this land he was mistaken for an Egyptian rather than identified as an Israelite, but Moses didn't mind. It was safer to perpetuate the lie rather than be who he was created to be.

In this place he could almost forget who he really was, and focused on scratching out a new life in the attempt to disassociate from his past. Exodus 2:21 reveals how disconnected from his true identity he'd become. We read Moses was *content* to dwell there in that place. His awareness had grown dull. His longings were suppressed. He was in comfortable captivity, and God let him stay there for forty years.

Moses had a wife and children, responsibilities and work, all of the usual things in life serving as both blessing and distraction. He kept busy with a normal life, or so he thought. His strategy of escape appeared to have worked. After all, he was in control…he'd preserved his own life and advanced his own agenda. But had he? In rare moments of painful honesty with himself, he wondered if this was really his destiny. Watching a bunch of sheep belonging to his father-in-law, day in and day out, was less than fulfilling. But it was a living.

Moses' deeper passions had long been stifled. The yearning for more had been set aside. His inborn fervor for justice and the desire to advocate for deliverance of the oppressed had been safely abandoned. Passion had proven to be a dangerous thing. He knew this far too well as he kept the emotion buried year after year. Just keep your head low, play it safe and do the best you can; these were the thoughts that played over and over.

I think you and I may be able to relate.

Like us, Moses could have easily believed he'd been forgotten, or been defined and limited by his past. Little did Moses know at the time that, even while in the wilderness, God was still at work. You see, Moses' mission, just like ours, had been ordained prior to the moment of his conception. The story was still being written. The plan hadn't been changed and Moses' purpose hadn't been given to someone else. His desert experience was all calculated as preparation for the greater epic to be told.

> Like us, Moses could have easily believed he'd been forgotten, or been defined and limited by his past.

Finally, when Moses was around eighty, the date of the unanticipated divine appointment came. The plot thickened as an unsuspecting Moses awakened to "normal" as he had been doing for so long. But this day was ordained as one he would remember. It was the day when his legacy was orchestrated to impact millions of lives then, now, and for the ages to come.

A Divine Appointment with the God Who Identifies Us

We read in Exodus chapter three the story of how on a day that started like any other, God revealed Himself to Moses. And as if that encounter were not life altering enough, God also outlined a divine rescue mission He intended Moses to lead.

Here is the overview of how it occurred. After getting Moses' attention with a burning bush that never burned up, Moses responded to hearing his name being called. "Here am I," he replied while hiding his face in fear as God gave a discourse of Himself and His plan. After it became clear that God intended to send him back into the heart of everything he thought he'd escaped so many years before, he spoke up. His beginning question for dialogue with God: "Who am I?"

And so it goes in our lives when God brings us to a place of divine encounter. You can be certain we will find ourselves with the same question upon our hearts as He draws us into a conversation with Himself. "Who am I, Lord God?" This inquiry serves as a spring board to deeper exploration of our hearts. It's the examination that needs completed prior to participating in our own exodus to freedom.

Moses' dialogue with God is recorded in Exodus chapters three and four and outlines the framework of the questions of our soul. Within the passage are five questions we ask of God during the process of coming to fuller recognition of the truth about our identity:

- Who am I?
- Who is my authority and by what power will I assert my purpose?
- What is my source of strength & credibility?
- What about my human frailties and imperfections—don't they get in the way of your plan?
- Are you sure you don't want to use someone else to write this story?

Do these questions sound familiar? Have you ever questioned who you really are, your worth, your ability, your preparation, your credibility, your power to overcome the enemy, your power to overcome sin and the world? And ultimately have you questioned, just as Moses questioned,

God's intentional decision to use a flawed vessel to deliver a message of importance?

Incredibly, God's utilization of broken vessels is a consistent theme. It is part of our mission, just like it was for Moses. We are called to deliver a message of hope and deliverance to those in captivity. We've been given the plan and the resources to execute the great escape. But first, we have to get through our questions…

So how did God respond to Moses, and how does He respond to us asking, "Who am I?" Like all great teachers, God answers a question with a question. He inquires, "Who do you believe I Am?" Who we believe the "I Am" to be is inextricably connected to whether we will find the clarity of knowing ourselves or not. Just like God answered Moses' identity concerns, He answers ours. He assures us that He's seen the details of our life. He knows the affliction and sorrows of his people.

> Who we believe the "I Am" to be is inextricably connected to whether we will find the clarity of knowing ourselves or not.

Taskmasters of emptiness also oppress us. They desire to inflict false answers in response to our identity question. "No one of value," they will tell us. "Only created as an object for another's purpose," they may sneer. "Fearful…dejected… sinner. Trapped by your own bad decisions, you idiot," they laugh. Isolated…the owner of a futile life…alone…unknown and forgotten. Far too often, we simply accept these answers and let them define our normal.

Have you ever experienced the barrage of these thoughts or felt the sting of these deceitful lies upon your soul? While in the desert of preparation, labels may be imposed on us by others and accepted by us as truth. But when we encounter God, He directs us to answer our question of identity and worthiness by looking to, or beholding Him.

He reminds us that it is *He* who created us and is with us. All design questions are to be referred back to the manufacturer. To alleviate our fears God boldly proclaims that He *is* the I AM. He is the Ever Existent One *who is defined by Himself, being Himself.*

God brings into focus that it is *His* very being and presence, and *His* calling upon us, which identifies us and gives us worth. *Whose* I am, answers who I am. Your acceptance that He is your Creator with an intended purpose for your life will initiate a confident awareness of your true identity and value. Ponder these weighty thoughts with me and allow them to permeate your heart.

You and I, as individuals, are *chosen* to be His. We *are worthy* because He (the Great I Am) has decreed it to be so. He has *designed* us with every detail of our *unique individuality* in mind. God is lovingly drawing us to a deeper encounter and greater intimacy as we behold who we are as created by Him.

> God is lovingly drawing us to a deeper encounter and greater intimacy as we behold who we are as created by Him.

I Am Made in the Image of God

And so how can we apply this? What is your true identity, the identity bestowed upon you by your Creator? For the answer, we briefly go back to the beginning. God determined in his omnipotence to make mankind in His image and likeness, giving them dominion to exercise and a mission to execute.

> *So God created man in his own image, in the image of God created he him; male and female created he them.* (Genesis 1:26-28)

Adam and Eve were created as image bearers of the Most High God, the Creator of the universe. Adam manifested God's power and strength to bring the Creator glory. Eve was the pinnacle of creation, a crown of adornment and honor, perfectly designed to complement her counterpart for the glory of God. As a woman, Eve manifested the exquisiteness and grace of creation displaying the attributes of God's captivating beauty. Together, as a power couple, Adam and Eve magnified the name of their Designer. Entirely complete in their uniquely ordained individuality and in relationship with God, they were to accomplish His mission together. They were the perfect pair showcasing the perfect image of God in a perfect environment.

But then almost everything changed.

Thankfully, some things are immutable, like God and His original intention. His plan was delayed, but not destroyed. Part of this plan is the fixed intent for men and women to magnify and manifest His glory to a watching world. The Creator's blueprint for us lived on in the divine strategy of His perfect heart.

God's Divine Blueprint

One role model, no matter your gender, is found in Proverbs. She is known as the virtuous woman. Her noble character qualities exemplify those to which both men and women should aspire. And while you, like me, may have been left to feel inferior after studying this person in the past, let's be encouraged by the truth. The truth is, if it were left up to you and me in our fallen human nature, this model could never be attained. Thankfully, when surrendered to the power of Christ, it isn't up to us any longer. We can rest in His work and His nature in us.

Among many other exceptional qualities, this person demonstrates six key attributes which set her apart from others.

- She's a *leader*—one that takes initiative and executes the plan
- She's an *advocate and intercessor*—one who rises to meet the needs of others without neglect to self
- She's a visionary *strategist*—one who sees possibility, then plans & executes
- She's *known for excellence*—one who allows her actions to speak without self-promotion; she excels many others who are said to have "done virtuously"
- She is *secure in her identity*—one who fears the Lord; identity isn't placed in fleeting exterior appearances

Think about it or refer back to compare. The contrast between this person and the Proverbs seven woman discussed in the last chapter is vast. One depicts who we are in our fallen nature, and the other is the person we were created to be in God's image. It is possible to live as the person we are fully created to be. But it isn't by focusing on the tasks listed in Proverbs thirty-one like you might think.

Greater effort, getting up earlier and staying up later won't do it. Biting your tongue and enduring it all with a smile is not the answer. In all the trying harder we only end up feeling like failures because of attempting the impossible in our own strength. We are ill-equipped in our human nature to be someone who bears the image of Christ.

And this is the whole point. Accomplishing tasks and modifying your behavior in an attempt to look more like the virtuous woman isn't the key to your identity. And that's a relief, is it not?

Key to Real Identity: Focus on Being—Not Doing

Despite what you may have been told by some well-meaning person in the past, *trying to clean up your life by attempting to adopt virtuous characteristics is not the key.* In fact, if you're able to be honest, you will have noticed that your human efforts of "trying" to clean up, shape up and get up, usually lead to giving up. Behavior modification is not the solution—internal transformation is. All of the focus on our exterior appearance and what others see is, in the end, futile.

Here's a foundational truth if we are to ever understand who we are: We must *be* not *do* to fully become the person God designed us to be. Read that again and internalize it. God originally designed us to *be* amazing creatures blessed with the beauty of His image and the insight of His wisdom to live a life of meaning. We are human *beings.* And as such, we were to be life-givers positively influencing and blessing all those within our circle of influence. But we live out of a corrupted identity far too often. How then can you transform and live more fully in the identity designed for you?

First, you must surrender any notion that *being* someone is the same as *doing* some things. The flawed notion that trying harder (doing) will produce a metamorphosis must be abandoned. Remember, *who you are, is not the same as what you do.* For instance, my roles as wife, mom, daughter, nurse, teacher, consultant, author, speaker, etc.... are not who I am, they are what I do. This means that while they provide the structure defining certain relationships and responsibilities for which I am accountable, I am a separate being apart from any of those roles.

> The flawed notion that trying harder (doing) will produce a metamorphosis must be abandoned.

Who you are helps define *how* you do what each of your roles requires. But if you define yourself merely by your roles, you are destined for heartache and emptiness when roles change. Our validation and purpose do not reside within any role other than as an image bearer of Jesus Christ, an ambassador of His kingdom. A child of God. When we behold Him, we behold the image of whom we are to conform. And therein is the power of transformation.

Key to Real Identity: Understand Virtue as Power— Desire the Force That Inspires Real Change

When I gained insight into the word "virtuous" I received a second key to unlock the concept of my real identity and behold who God designed me to be. This word describing the woman in Proverbs 31:10 is the Hebrew word *chayil*. Interestingly, in other places within Scripture, this word is more frequently translated as army, valor, valiant, force, strength and power.[1]

Virtuous is actually a word communicating something much different from that which I had been taught over the years by well-meaning teachers. In the past when studying this person, speakers would define virtue as moral goodness, righteousness and chastity, making these the predominant focus. While these are important character qualities, the failure to look at the root word obscured a much richer and relevant meaning. This person was actually a force with which to contend. She displayed valor and strength to accomplish her mission, fighting a battle that matters.

Now this interests me; does it you?

This person possesses a confident power and knows how to use it for good. Consequently, she does many good things with people's best interest at heart. She is valiant and inspires others. Her life has purpose and meaning. She's living her life with positive impact as intended. Something on the inside makes her an exception to the status quo.

So how can we too live like this? What is the secret to having real strength and influence, as opposed to manipulative control? The answer is found in Proverbs 31:30. This verse explains the differences between two types of people: the virtuous woman and another person described in verse twenty-nine. It's a comparison of two people who closely resemble each other, but are very different.

> *Many daughters have done virtuously, but you excel them all. Favor is deceitful and beauty is vain: but a woman that fears the Lord, she shall be praised.*

It's a small nuance in communication, but did you catch it? Should we be content as one who's described as having "done virtuously?" After all, nice people do a lot of virtuous things. Nice people do virtuously by working the nursery week after week at church, raising money for social justice causes and a myriad of other volunteer and community service activities. How could there be anything better said of a person than, "they always behaved virtuously?"

Who is it that excels? The scripture delivers our answer.

Doing Virtuously Versus Being Virtuous

While some may stay busy scrambling to "do virtuously," the key to becoming the person of virtue is not in focusing on the "doing" of nice things. Claiming your original divine design as God intended is tied to one distinguishing choice. It is connected to one motivating factor, and it's not to build a resume of benevolence to impress yourself or others with the number of good things accomplished.

The person of virtue is a person of power, driven by a heavenly agenda. The key is the choice to fear the Lord. There's no underlying motive to attain the attention, approval, or accolades of other people. The fear of the Lord is the only motivation. But you may ask, "Isn't that concept a bit archaic?" My response is that God is the same yesterday, today and forever. As an eternal being He has neither beginning nor end. God is both archaic and contemporary. He and His Word are completely relevant no matter the era.

So what exactly is the fear of the Lord? It's a subject not often spoken of in many contemporary Christian circles, although the scriptures have much to say about it. A healthy reverence and respect for God, Who has power over the soul and the body as explained in Matthew 10:25 is part of it, but a relationship based out of fear in this sense is not what God is seeking to have with you and me. The fear of the Lord addresses your deepest *desires*.

God wants you to *want* Him. The Creator of the universe wants a relationship based in love and desire—not duty. Scripture firmly ties the concept of the fear of the Lord to an attitude of heart that respects and loves God and the manifestation of Himself, the Word, above all else. The fear of the Lord leads to the uninhibited desire to know God intimately.

So in the process of grasping our full identity as virtuous woman and men designed by God to live powerful lives as His witnesses, we must learn to fear the Lord if we wish to excel. Scripture defines the fear of the Lord as the beginning of knowledge and wisdom. In addition it is to hate evil, pride, arrogance, the evil way and deceitful talk.[2]

Proverbs 2:1-5 teaches how to obtain understanding of this attitude of heart. All of the required actions involve a matter of our will and the intentional purpose to know God through His Word: receive...memorize...meditate...

listen...ask...seek...search. And then, succinctly stated in Ecclesiastes 12:13, we read that our *whole duty* is tied to the fear of the Lord and what we do with His Word.

> *Let us hear the conclusion of the whole matter: Fear God and keep His commandments: for this is the whole duty of man.*

Do you see the key point of application? Instead of focusing on merely *doing* truly nice, virtuous activities, our life focus is to get to know our Creator and Redeemer in authentic intimacy as we seek Him with tenacity and diligence. It is only by knowing and loving the Word that we will have the correct motives to do virtuous things that fulfill our divine duty.

When we see God for who He is, we are able to become who God designed us to be. In our true identity in Christ, we can deliver life, rather than death and dispense wisdom rather than drivel. Our life can declare truth rather than deceit, thereby becoming exceptional...virtuous.

Actions become true manifestations of one's desire for God and the fruit of intimacy with Him when we fear the Lord, rather than acting out of duty. The fear of the Lord draws you and me to our divine source of strength and wisdom. It enables us to become all we were created to be: virtuous and powerful, exemplifying authentic beauty. The beauty of God within us, reaching out to captivate the attention of a world hungry for His healing and transforming touch.

Behold Who You Authentically Are

You are God's beautiful creation and are part of His plan. And beauty, as a matter of the innermost heart, not just the exterior, is a powerful attribute when beheld. To behold something is much more than to look casually at it.

Consider the historical evolution of the word "behold" from its root meaning, "to hold." Biblically its usage bids the listener to pay close attention; it's a word punctuating the message to be delivered by the speaker meaning, *"to know, to see"*—*"fix the eyes upon, perceive, discern, cherish."*[3] In other words, pay close attention and focus.

> You are God's beautiful creation and are part of His plan.

Our focus defines our thoughts and inner attitudes. Beholding beauty is to focus on a timeless, thus divine attribute. And while society has corrupted the way most people define beauty, the world's version is just a cheap perversion to divert and deflect the truth.

Real beauty is a force of the Almighty. It inspires, nurtures and refreshes—beauty gives life. When we as Christians fail to behold ourselves as beautiful creations of God, complete in Christ as redeemed, we limit the power of God within us. Failure to behold God's beauty within us is the root cause of not knowing who we are. When we truly behold Him we will showcase our identity in Him.

Whether displayed by nature around us, or manifested by His love within us, real beauty in His creation manifests the Creator and calls those who behold it to see Him. *"Oh worship the Lord in the beauty of holiness."* (Psalm 96:9a) Beauty captivates the observer and invokes desire, adoration and worship. But the power of beauty can be exploited, just as it as it was by the beautiful creature, Lucifer, in ages past.[4]

Satan knows who we really are even if we do not. He understands the threat we represent as daughters and sons of the King of Kings if we display our Creator's beauty. He knows that if we ever grasped our true identity we would be a force with which to contend. Far too often as a norm, we allow the enemy to steal what is rightfully ours because we do not understand who we are.

Many Christians continue settling for powerless lives because they are still living an illusion of the false-self. They're still chained by the fog of confusion. Remember, our enemy is incredibly jealous of our position with God. Lucifer's original role was to magnify the Creator and proclaim the glory of the Lord through worship. He was to use his beauty to captivate attention and direct all eyes to the glory of God. But he blew it because of his pride and now doesn't want God's glory magnified through you and me either.

If he can keep you and me in bondage to the power of sin and deceit, he nullifies the power of the beauty of Christ within us. And he is successful, far too often.

Our lives are to sing a grand story, like an opera raising its beautiful strains to the glory of God. Consider now, is your life singing? Or has your voice been silenced by the enemy? To thrive, we must allow our life story to carol praise to our Creator and Savior. When we behold our God and see our real identity because of Him, we understand the privilege of magnifying His name.

Take a deep breath, my friend, and lift up your voice.

Exceed in life and become exceptional.

Let new vitality fill your lungs as you *behold Him.*

Then see your own beautiful, beloved identity and impact this hurting world with your song of redemption.

KEYS TO THRIVE

Embrace Your Real Identity.

1) What does the following statement mean in your life personally? "We must focus on *being* rather than merely *doing* to be the person God created us to be." *Stop. Surrender. Listen only to + for Hs voice. Move only when He directs*

2) The fear of the Lord is the key to becoming the person of strength and influence as you were designed to be. Do you receive God's word and listen intently as you cry after knowledge and seek understanding as silver—mining the truth diligently? (Review Proverbs 2:1-11) *I believe I do!*

3) Colossians 2:9-10 teaches us some important truths about ourselves as Christians. How important is it for you to know you are complete and perfect—lacking nothing in Christ? *Wow— we have everything in us!!*

4) 2 Peter 1:2-4 teaches some powerful truths for us to internalize: A) Grace and peace is *multiplied* unto you (not mere addition) through the knowledge of God and Jesus Christ. B) His divine power has given you <u>*all things*</u> pertaining unto life and godliness. C) We have been called to glory and virtue (virtue=power, excellence.) How is your

personal insight of the Christian life revolution-
ized by these truths? *It's all something we
have NOW*

5) Truth to ponder: Colossians 2:9-10; 2 Peter 1:2-4;
Galatians 5:1; Philippians 1:6

---

* For additional resources on discovering
your identity in Christ visit
kayemcarter.com/setfreetothrive/resources

PART THREE

DISCOVER LIFE THAT THRIVES

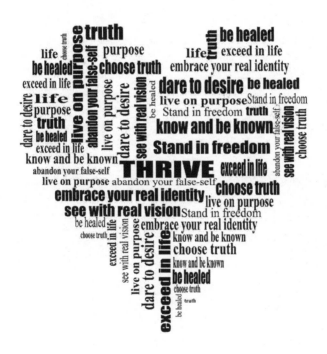

7

I MUST BE ABOUT SOMETHING

Do You Know Why You Are Here?

*We had to learn...that it did not really matter what we expected
from life, but rather what life was expecting from us.*

Viktor Frankl, *Man's Search for Meaning*

One of the deepest questions of the soul is about
purpose. To fully thrive we need solid answers to
the question, "Why was I born?" To be set free
from fear, you must understand what the story of your life
is about and that your life *matters*. Wired deep within us by
our Creator, we each have an inherent need for meaning.
Viktor Frankl, an Austrian neurologist, psychiatrist and
World War II concentration camp survivor witnessed how
this fulfilled or unfulfilled need for meaning played out in
his own life and the lives of countless others.

In *Man's Search for Meaning*, he details life in a Nazi
death camp and shares the spiritual lessons learned during
unimaginable suffering and injustice. Importantly, he noted

how those who lost their sense of meaning or hope died quickly. Others exceeded the norm; they survived. The German philosopher Nietzsche's said, "He who has a *why* to live for can bear almost any *how*."[1] Frankl exemplified this to a degree most will never understand.

> "…Often it is just such an exceptionally difficult external situation which gives man the opportunity to grow spiritually beyond himself. Instead of taking the camp's difficulties as a test of their inner strength, [*some*] did not take their life seriously and despised it as something of no consequence… Life for such people became meaningless."[2]

Your *why* is of critical importance, enabling you to survive the *how* of your life. This includes a life story incorporating a Nazi concentration camp, or one full of other seemingly unfair circumstances beyond your control. Perhaps you've endured abuse, betrayals, divorce, illness, the death of a child, the diagnosis of terminal disease or just general disappointments. Your reason for living must be clearly known to you, or you face the peril of losing hope during life's trials. You'll risk succumbing to an outlook that life is pointless.

Knowing the purpose for which we exist is mission-critical. Without it, people mentally quit when encountering hardship. All savvy business leaders understand this to anticipate and counteract resistance to change. Countless resources are spent to ensure that team members understand the mission to which their efforts contribute. Military leaders certainly know the importance of inspiring troops by defining the mission. It's the foundation of any strategy and provides the power to press on in the fight.

> Knowing the purpose for which we exist is mission-critical.

But in a world of greater access to information and improved technology, our inner awareness has become more dim. Most people continue to struggle with truly knowing their purpose. They spend a lifetime looking without clearly finding the "something" that validates their existence.

And regrettably, this applies to Christians as well. Instead of living intentionally and purposefully, people of faith also struggle to really know why they are here. But knowing your purpose, coupled with your real identity will stabilize your soul. Together they define the trajectory of your life.

Following Truth is Mission-Critical

Let's take a look at one who viewed His identity and purpose with perfect clarity. He knew the goal and understood He'd been launched to squarely hit the target while living His story on earth. He was completely focused and mission driven. He knew "what he was about" demonstrating that He knew the vision for His life at the young age of twelve. His name is Jesus.

Luke 2:40-52 records insight into special distinctions about the disposition of Jesus as a boy. In a story about what could have seemed like a very typical interaction regarding miscommunication or misunderstanding between an adolescent and his parents, the reader is invited to look deeper into more than that which met the eye.

After "getting left behind" in Jerusalem following his family's attendance at at the Passover celebration, Jesus is found by his worried parents in the temple conversing with the religious academics of the day. We read that all who

SET FREE TO THRIVE

heard him were astonished at his deep understanding and articulate answers. He was recognized already as one who was different, He exceeded the norm.

When Jesus was confronted by his mother for worrying her, He made a very profound and atypical statement found in Luke 2:49, which I paraphrase below. His answer led Mary to ponder, as it does us as well.

> *"Why were you looking for me? Didn't you know I must be about my Father's business?"*

I am relatively certain that when confronted about causing you worry, your son (or any twelve year old boy you may encounter) is much like mine was. They don't typically respond like Jesus did. And if they do feign some highly philosophical or spiritual posture, it quickly unravels into peals of laughter at your raised eyebrow and look of quizzical disbelief. While young adolescents are beginning to look for answers to questions pertaining to who they are and how they fit-in, most don't spend a whole lot of time in deep introspection.

In my experience, kids (and most adults too) must be drawn, and sometimes prodded into deeper thinking. Most are not methodically calculating the path their life will take. But Jesus' words and actions clearly demonstrated the depth of his insight. He knew the two most important concepts that define the direction and impact of a life: one's identity and purpose.

The trajectory of His life was declared even as His words reassured his earthly parents. Jesus knew who He was and that He was on a special mission. Most importantly, *He knew who He was because He knew who His Father was.* He was connected to His Father as part of the Trinity for all of eternity and proclaimed His own identity when He referred to *His Father.* His clarity defined the direction the story His life would take. And this is true for our lives as well.

Knowing our Father and our role in His business will define the direction of our lives.

What Is the Story of Your Life About?

Jesus' simple statement: *"I must be about my Father's business,"* revealed his clear insight into His life's purpose. *He* as an individual, *was about* His Father's business. Succinct and to the point, He shared His mission statement, the summary of His life before the story completely unfolded. His life had eternal impact because He didn't allow himself to become distracted from that which He knew was His mission and *His* mission alone.

We will know the joy of the crown set before us in the face of enduring the cross when we too come to know our personal mission and have vision for the eternal. When we determine to define the summary of our life story before it completely unfolds, we are on the path to fulfillment and meaning. Setting our sight on a higher dimension and coming to understand our eternal purpose keeps us on course, despite life-altering circumstance.

How would you answer if someone were to ask you, "So what are you about?" My prayer is for you to be able to answer confidently and with intention. But we must plot the trajectory of our lives through the clarity and vision of Christ. We all long at the deepest level to know we live powerful lives of impact. We desire to know with certainty who we are and then operate in security because of *knowing what we are about.* But knowing our purpose in

> Setting our sight on a higher dimension and coming to understand our eternal purpose keeps us on course, despite life-altering circumstance.

Christ is only possible when we transcend the superficial and irrelevant.

My vision of the larger goal stabilized my heart and mind in the midst of chaos many times over. Even in my darkest days, *the clarity of my purpose on the eternal continuum served to disrupt the inertia of my fall.* A view of my eternal purpose shifted the angle of my sight and changed the momentum, enabling me to get back up.

You and I are to live *on purpose*, not by random default, haphazardly tossed by winds of circumstance. Let's focus now on defining our mission, the purpose for which we were created. As with so many other things, we will find the keys to understanding by going back to the beginning.

The Framework of Our Purpose

> *"And God said, Let us make man **in our image**, after our likeness: and **let them have dominion** over...all the earth...so male and female created He them. And God blessed them, and said unto them, **Be fruitful, and multiply**, and replenish the earth, and subdue it."* (Genesis 1:26-28, emphasis mine)

In this passage we find the keys to fulfillment as we discover what we were originally purposed to accomplish. It is only by living within *our designed purpose that we will experience joy and fulfillment in the real meaning of our lives.* The framework of this mission is made up of three components outlined in the Scripture. They are easily remembered by visualizing what I call the Mission Triangle.

This figure has three points representing three distinct but related elements: multiply, minister, manifest. The absence of even one point on a triangle removes a vital component required for its existence. In like manner, the integrity of our own mission is fulfilled only by preserving the cohesion of all three parts. An incomplete triangle, lacking even one point, wouldn't fulfill the requirements for being a triangle. Consequently, the deficit might leave the structure to be described as *unfulfilled.*

Likewise, we'll only find complete fulfillment in recognition and surrender to our triune purpose, as ordained by a triune God. We are to multiply, minister, and manifest. If you intentionally build your life on this original-design framework, you'll become fulfilled, or *filled full* in your divine purpose. You'll find the answer to your why.

Multiply

First, our original purpose includes an element of reproduction, to give and to nurture life. Having physical children and raising them has been one of the most rewarding aspects of my life personally, but being a mother does not define my purpose. You too accomplish your mission through the conduit of various roles you may have, but you must remember: *your roles are not the same as your purpose.*

God's instruction to multiply was about much more than simply having physical offspring to populate the earth. Remember the context. At the time of this conversation recorded in Genesis, Adam and Eve hadn't chosen to sin. They still existed in the perfect image of God, radiating His glory as spiritually alive beings, living in perfect harmony with Him and each other.

God wanted to expand the family and expand the glory of His kingdom. Adam and Eve were commissioned to initiate that process. They were to reproduce children who were spiritually alive—not dead. Their mission could have been accomplished because sin wasn't a barrier in their world at the time. But as you know, it did not end up happening that way.

Thankfully we know God had the master plan under control. His strategy included a personal remedy for the spiritual death now passed on from our first mother and father. It's because of this strategy that we receive a similar charge in the New Testament. Jesus declares in John 15:16,

> "...I have chosen you and ordained you, that you should go and bring forth fruit, and that your fruit should remain."

You and I are called to something more fulfilling than the temporary and physical. He calls us to join Him and grasp what we were called and ordained to do; something that has eternal, lasting value because of Jesus' victory on the cross.

Later, as paraphrased below, the apostle Paul teaches by using the metaphor of marriage in Romans 7:4. He encourages believers in Christ to understand they are no longer bound to the Old Testament law for their salvation and ongoing acceptance by God.

"… You are dead to the law by the body of Christ; that you should be married to another, even to Him who is raised from the dead, that we should bring forth fruit unto God."

We again are shown the important component of multiplication, bearing fruit for God's glory through an intimate relationship. Our charge to multiply has much deeper and broader implications than merely bringing physical children into this world. I hope you see clearly that we are called, thus have a mission, to bring new life spiritually into this world. You and I are to destroy the effects of death and chaos by becoming co-contributors of life with God. We are called to advance the cause of Christ, increasing the scope of God's kingdom as we invest in others the new life we have received from Him.

> You and I are to destroy the effects of death and chaos by becoming co-contributors of life with God.

To fulfill your mission to multiply, you must be a life-giver by bearing the fruit of an intimate relationship with God. *If you are really serious about fulfilling your personal mission you must become intimate, not merely remain a casual acquaintance with Jesus.* There is no other way to bear enduring fruit in our lives. Drawing others to come to know and thrive in a relationship with Christ is one of our highest privileges. Multiplying His image in the world bears witness to His life in us.

Minister

The second component within our framework of purpose is to minister. What does this mean for you? Typically, we think first of full-time vocational pastors as ministers. It's a minister's job, to minister, right? But the word minister is a noun *and* a verb. And as a verb, it is an action that all Christians can, and more importantly are called to do.

As we explore the meaning of ministry as outlined in Genesis, think about the word "administer." Administration requires dominion. It's the scope of influence given to each person as stewards. God mentioned dominion twice in our passage from Genesis. He first said, "Let them have dominion," and He then defined the scope of this administrative power as the whole earth and every living creature upon it. God then repeated Himself, giving command to "subdue" the earth. To subdue is to have dominion, thus God-given work is to administer God-given power within the scope given to each of us.

Let that sink in. Part of your purpose is to *minister* or ad*minister* the dominion you've been given as an image-bearer of God. Accomplishing God-given, fulfilling work is part of our purpose. Doing purposeful work satisfies a God-given basic human need. If you remove meaning and trade it for mere busyness, the inner drive of a soul slowly fades.

But the key for meaningful work is in personal perspective, not in the actual mechanics of the task or vocation. I once heard a story that demonstrates this well. A man came to a busy worksite and asked a laboring man what he was doing. With furrowed eyebrows and a tone of annoyance the worker replied, "I am laying bricks!" The curious man moved on to another laborer who also appeared to be laying bricks, yet

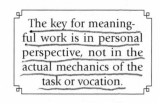

The key for meaningful work is in personal perspective, not in the actual mechanics of the task or vocation.

who was whistling a cheerful tune. "What are you doing," the inquisitive man asked? The worker replied happily, "I am building a cathedral!"

Each laborer was doing the same thing. Yet one found meaning and joy in the midst of that which appeared mundane and valueless to the other. One recognized the magnitude of his mission and saw the big picture. The other was lost sourly in the burden of the tasks, just going through the motions of life to get by. The difference was their focus. Only one transcended the hardship of the moment. He saw the vision of something greater and counted it a privileged to contribute.

You and I are encouraged by the apostle Paul in Ephesians chapter four to walk worthy of the vocation in which we are called. But in context this passage deals with far more than bricklaying. He invites us to see life and our life's work with the greater vision: to see the cathedral, built up together as we advance the cause of Christ.

We have been made able ministers of the New Testament, reconciled to God through Jesus Christ, now given the *ministry* of reconciliation through the *word* of reconciliation.[3] Part of our purpose is to work, ministering as stewards the life we have been given. We are privileged to be builders and co-contributors to an eternal kingdom.

Manifest

The last element of the divine framework of purpose is revealed by His intent to make man in His image. To make or reveal the image of God is to manifest it, to cause something once obscured to become apparent or evident. So what should we expose as divine image bearers of our creative God? As Christians, we possess the divine energy of creation within us. Consequently, we are to release this power of Light into a world of chaos, pushing back the darkness.

Remember how chaos, the great void, was dispelled by God back in Genesis 1:1? We are now privileged as His image bearers to reveal Light and produce a similar effect. As Christians we are to make manifest in our mortal life the eternal life of Jesus.[4] The purpose of the human life of Jesus is clearly defined in 1 John 3:8,

> As Christians we are to make manifest in our mortal life the eternal life of Jesus.

> *"For this purpose the Son of God was manifested, that he might destroy the works of the devil."*

If Jesus' purpose was to destroy the works of the enemy, and we are to manifest the power of Jesus in our lives, we too must seek to destroy the works of the devil.

In Acts 26:18 Paul explains his own purpose:

> *"To open their eyes and to turn them from darkness to light, and from the power of Satan unto God…"*

Manifesting the image of Christ in your life means you are involved in the ministry of Christ, the ministry of reconciliation. We are to showcase Him to a world He loved enough to die for. His image shining through you will advance His ministry as recorded in Luke 4:18. In this passage he made the purpose of his mission clear: *He had come to proclaim the good news, heal the brokenhearted, deliver the captive, recover sight to the blind and set-free the wounded.* There is nothing more rewarding than to minister real healing and freedom to a broken, captive soul.

We have the privilege of being a part of the process when we stay connected to Christ. This ability to magnify Christ in our lives as we multiply and minister is only possible through the power of God. Jesus expounds in John 15:4-5:

> *"Abide in me, and I in you. As the branch cannot bear fruit of itself, except it abide in the vine; no more can you, except you abide in me. I am the vine, you are the branches: He that abides in me, and I in him, the same brings forth much fruit: **for without me you can do nothing.**"* (emphasis mine)

Unless we abide in Christ, that is, unless we stay connected like a branch to the sustaining vine—we cannot multiply, we cannot minister, and we cannot manifest His image. Without Him, it is impossible to accomplish our mission, living a fulfilling life of purpose as divinely designed. The person attempting to live a life apart from an intimate relationship with Christ will live in the bondage of chaos because what they do is in their own strength. These well-intended people of faith fail to live the abundant life Jesus came to give.

And this sadly describes far too many of us. Just like nonbelievers, Christians go through the motions of living, doing the best they can while hoping for an eventual breakthrough. Many are nice people doing nice things. They attend church, tithe, volunteer, teach a class, have titles, and try to be "good." Many even know a lot about the Bible.

But, without authentically abiding in Christ all of the doing is undone and it counts as nothing. Any of our work done in our own power only glorifies us, not Christ. It will yield no reward for eternity. It does not fulfill our mission. Only endeavors making it through the fire of truth at the judgment seat of Christ will endure.[5] As a Christian do you wish to have lived a life that mattered—knowing you lived the mission Christ gave to you as an individual? If so, it is time to get serious and focus.

→ Define Your Mission

I ask you to begin prayerfully considering your personal mission. How have you been uniquely equipped and called to multiply, minister and manifest? What desire has He placed in your heart? Ask the Lord to give you your answer as you ask Him: "What is my mission, Lord? What do you want to accomplish uniquely through me?" How have you been preparing me throughout this story of my life?"

Writing a personal mission statement is important for at least three reasons:

- It forces introspection & self-evaluation
- It provides focus during chaotic periods of battle
- It provides ongoing clarity for setting and modifying goals and tactics as you live intentionally instead of haphazardly

Here is a tip to get started. Prayerfully ask the Lord to help you fill in the blank:

I exist to _____ *worship Him & serve others*.

Your mission statement is one sentence; think about each word to make it clear and as concise as possible. It will represent a personal proclamation from God to you. For instance, mine is: "I exist to be a witness of the Truth." How I do this becomes the framework for my personal tactics.

Defining your mission provides the basis for certainty in decision-making. It helps you differentiate what gets the "yes," and what gets the "no." Living on mission and knowing your purpose rids you of false-guilt for saying no to things that simply do not fit in the framework. You will experience the benefit of greater peace in this chaotic, frenzied world when you can set boundaries to preserve your emotional and physical energy.

Greater vision to execute your mission comes as each chapter of your life's story unfolds. You'll recognize that your story, although still in the context of war, is part of our King's grander story and His plan for the ages. We are called and blessed to take part in this epic saga that will endure beyond time and into eternity. It's only within this context that we find our designed purpose.

While for years I had known the need to be mission-oriented, it wasn't until I personally experienced the terror of battle that I began to comprehend its critical nature. I didn't have complete clarity until the firefight around me left me in a position of utter dependence and without any illusion of control.

I exist to do the will of Him who gave me new life, surrendering my story to be written about Him. And now I encourage you to do the same.

Define and then execute your mission, manifesting the glory of God with your own life.

Refuse a default mode existence which leads to a life stamped: "Mission Cancelled."

Exceed in life: live zealously, refusing the status quo of this world.

Be about your Father's business.

"See that you walk circumspectly, not as fools, but as wise, redeeming the time because the days are evil. Therefore, don't be unwise, but understand what the will of the Lord is." (Ephesians 5:15-17)

KEYS TO THRIVE

Live on Purpose.

1) Has your life purpose up until now been more about your own business, (your humanly driven desires) or the Father's business? My own

2) Think about how you can begin intentionally multiplying, ministering and manifesting Christ through your life story as perhaps never before. Think outside the box and consider the entire scope of your influence.

3) We can only live fulfilled lives, "filled full" of joy and peace when we abide in Christ—that is to know Him intimately, to be one with Him. What barriers to intimacy with God do you recognize in your own life?

4) Christ's purpose was manifested to destroy the works of the devil. (1 John 3:8) How has His purpose been revealed in your life story? After an encounter with Jesus, what in your story changed for your good and His glory? My Story

5) Truth to ponder: 1 Thessalonians 2:12; Romans 13:12; Ephesians 5:11; 1 Peter 2:9

8

DEFYING RELATIONAL CHAOS

Are You Able to Know and Be Known?

"To be fully known and truly loved...is like being loved by God."

Timothy Keller, *The Meaning of Marriage*

Our God is a relational God. He didn't spin the world into existence and then take a distant seat to observe from afar. He created you and I for relationships, first with Himself and then with others. A life full of vitality is one of thriving relationships built on substance. In this world of global connectivity and social media communities we remain hungry for real relationship because it's the essence of our existence. We were created for intimacy and authenticity, but far too often we settle for a surface deep sham in the exchange of selfies, longing to know and be known.

The need for authentic connections is a God-given need. Intimacy has been appropriately described as: *"in-to-me-see."* It's the place of transparently knowing and being known at the level of the heart without barriers. And as you likely know, it's rare and precious in this life between humans. In perfect form, it can only be known in a relationship with God, who already knows us better than we know ourselves.

> *To be loved but not known is comforting but superficial.*
>
> *To be known and not loved is our greatest fear. But to be fully known and truly loved…is like being loved by God. It is what we need more than anything.*
>
> *It liberates us from pretense, humbles us out of our self-righteousness, and fortifies us for any difficulty life can throw at us.”[1]*

Our deepest need for connection was intentionally placed within us as the void that can't be filled by anything or anyone but our Creator. Real intimacy cannot be attained without authenticity. In other words, without getting real and exposing ourselves, our need can't be met. When we decide to "get real" and drop the mask of the impostor (the false-self as discussed in chapter four) we expose ourselves to God, allowing for the deep connection for which we've been designed.

But intimacy is scary because we all have been wounded. It requires vulnerability, the naked exposure of the heart. Therefore, true intimacy involves risk. And risk is the reason a majority of people, both Christian and non-Christian, avoid true authenticity and real connections. You see, there is one inner need remaining in constant conflict with this need for intimacy; it is the need for safety.

So despite the fact that intimacy can also be exhilarating…energizing…liberating…and comforting, we bury the need and try to avoid the emptiness while playing it safe. But this unmet need for authentic connection continues to exert its power in the subconscious, impacting many human relational dysfunctions and our ability to contribute with healthy self-expression.

Only through abiding in close connection to Christ are we able to overcome our fear-based living and take off the mask with ourselves, God, and others. The freedom found in authenticity releases us from the game of "image management" as we relinquish the role of the impostor.

Learning to build healthy, authentic relationships is of utmost importance due to the magnitude of influence they have on our lives. Because of their importance we will explore quite a bit of detail in the coming pages. You and I need to explore our own relationships and understand more about how we personally relate to others in order to best position ourselves to thrive. Or relationships are crucial because they are the means by which we demonstrate God's love. Consequently, good relationships that glorify God are not haphazardly developed. They require intentional work based on a framework designed by God.

The Four Pillars of Healthy Relationships

Dysfunctional relating skills, like most other human sources of chaos tie back to a root cause: we fail to operate our lives according to the owner's manual, and many times, out of simply not knowing what we don't know. God gives a clear blueprint for building healthy relationships right from the beginning. I call them God's four pillars for healthy relationships. We will explore each truth and the chaos occurring when pillars are broken or missing.

Genesis 2:18 paraphrased below, teaches that God looked upon Adam's condition of being alone and proclaimed it "not good." But importantly, this wasn't because

He was incomplete, but because he couldn't accomplish God's mission to multiply by himself. God remedies the situation by creating Eve as an appropriate helper or partner for Adam.

> *And the LORD God said, It is not good that the man should be alone; I will make an appropriate helper for him.*

In this verse the first two pillars for healthy relationships and the basis for true intimacy are revealed in God's creative solution through Eve:

- Pillar One is *Shared Natures*—Healthy relationships are built with those of like-nature; true companionship is with others living spiritually alive in the image of God.

- Pillar Two is *Complementary Dispositions*—Healthy relationships are built with those who understand their individual role is *not to compete with, nor complete* the other.

Genesis 2:24-25 provides the truths for the next two pillars required:

> *"Therefore shall a man leave his father and his mother, and shall cleave unto his wife: and they shall be one flesh. And they were both naked, the man and his wife, and were not ashamed."*

- Pillar Three is the *Utilization of Healthy Boundaries*—Healthy relationships require leaving some and attaching to others.

- Pillar Four is the *Mutual Commitment to Authenticity*—Healthy relationships value and facilitate mutual exposure without fear.

Building with Shared Natures—Pillar One

The healthiest of relationships are built with those of like-nature. These are people who share your core values and beliefs and most importantly, your belief and faith in God. This belief in God isn't shallow intellectual awareness of a remote God somewhere out there, but a belief that truly impacts and changes lives. It's the faith that produces an alive spirit because of a personal relationship with God through His Son, Jesus.

Healthy relationships occur when two healthy, otherwise known as *alive,* individuals relate to one another out of the life they have been given through their relationship to God. Adam and Eve were both made in the image of God and alive spiritually as detailed in Genesis 1:27. They were able at that time to live intimately with God and each other, individually whole, holy and healthy people. This pillar, as the most important of the four, provides the deep footing necessary to build with the other three pillars.

Defying the Chaos of Relationships Lacking Shared Natures

Without having shared natures, people can't interact in complete transparency and true intimacy because at least one person is partially dead. While you and I have many relationships with many people who are either spiritually dead or those who act dead, these relationships are critically limited in depth and scope. Life cannot connect with death. This is one reason why some of your relationships feel so draining, so much like a ball and chain. Dead weight is a heavy burden.

I know many women who are married to wonderful men who provide for them and love them to the best degree possible as men without Christ. But each of the ladies will admit, their ability to connect in spiritual intimacy with their husband, thus in total intimacy, is a longing that can't be fulfilled without his personal relationship with Christ.

Consider these warnings I've paraphrased from scripture below. They help us understand with whom to form close connections. God knows how important our relationships are, and how they can influence our lives. His Word equips us with an abundance of wisdom for facilitating healthy relationships. We are commanded to love everyone as does Christ, but the people with whom we form attachments are limited by the following exhortations:

- *Do not bind yourself to one who is an unbeliever* [thus spiritually dead] *because there is no agreement between righteousness and unrighteousness and no communion between light and darkness.* (2 Corinthians 6:14)

- *Do not associate with anyone who calls himself a Christian* [thus claims to be spiritually alive] *who is sexually immoral, or greedy, or idolizes other things more than God, or is verbally abusive, or a drunkard or a swindler.* (1 Corinthians 5:11)

- *Withdraw yourself from anyone who calls themselves a Christian who walks disorderly* [in Greek this meant one who walks "out of rank, as a soldier;"[2] insubordinate to the commander] (2 Thessalonians 3:6)

- *Do not closely associate with this "out of rank soldier" so that he will feel ashamed* [and then get back in line]... *but do not count him as an enemy, warn or admonish him as a brother.* (2 Thessalonians 3:14 & 15)

God knows, as do we, that words are cheap. Anyone can claim to be a follower of Christ, or mistakenly call themselves a Christian because their parents were Christians or because they attend a church or partake in religious activity. God admonishes us to evaluate if the walk matches the talk. The pattern of a life, either reflecting or failing to reflect the life of Christ, is the telling factor.

Relationships with those *claiming* to be Christians, but who fail to live as Christ in their pattern of living, lack capacity for authenticity and intimacy. This is because at the level of the heart, values remain different. While you and I can never know another person's heart condition and spiritual position before God, we are taught in Matthew chapter twelve that like trees, people can be known by the fruit of their lives.

The level of relationship is limited if people don't demonstrate a genuine desire to follow God's Word as the *authority for all matters in life.* It's only by the Word living through us that we can sacrificially minister to each other's needs on all levels. Until death is exchanged for life people aren't whole. They simply can't contribute to the fullest health of the relationship. Only during the process of mutual transformation will a relationship between two people thrive in its fullest intended vigor.

> Only during the process of mutual transformation will a relationship between two people thrive in its fullest intended vigor.

Complementary Dispositions—Pillar Two

The healthiest of relationships are those built by people with mutually shared, spiritually alive natures, but these relationships don't just stand on one leg. Healthy relationships also require a second pillar of stability: individuals acknowledging the complementary role they are to play in the other's life.

Something is said to be complementary when it's combined with something different from itself to enhance the other. The two different and distinctly individual things become better when paired. Unique qualities of each are magnified and strengthened.

Simply stated, relationships made of individuals with complementary dispositions are "for" the other. A person with a complementary disposition is one who will seek to bring out the best in you. Two people in a complementary relationship desire the other to become all they were designed to be, sacrificially relating to one another to facilitate growth. These people look out for the best interest of the other person by building up, assisting, and supporting. Each helps the other; thereby both are encouraged to reach their own individual God-given potential.

I hope you have someone in your life complementing you. Currently, God has blessed me with a husband like this. He builds me up and supports me in countless ways on this journey of becoming who God created me to be. My husband sacrificially loves me, serving Christ as He looks out for my best interest. Despite us being complete opposites in many ways, we are able to complement one another for the glory of our Lord. I had no idea in my first marriage how to articulate it, but now I know this pillar was completely missing, and for a reason.

Only whole and emotionally healthy people can relationally complement or enhance others. Only those living out of the spiritual wholeness they have in Christ are truly set free to give without expectation, rather than living as a taker. The sad truth is that since many Christians haven't learned to live in their spiritual wholeness, they remain bound by the power of their old fallen nature; the part of them that's still ruled by inner insecurities.

Whether real or perceived, lack of safety and security will lead people to do many things in the attempt to diminish an emotional or spiritual void. Three inner fear-based beliefs plague the core of every heart in one degree or another: "I don't *have* enough," "I am *not loved* enough," and "*I* am not enough."[3] The drive to disprove these lies of our enemy leads people to desperate places. When we either seek to validate ourselves in our own power or numb the fear and pain that sustain the inner lies, we will be perpetually unable to complement others and give out of our abundance.

Defying the Chaos of Relationships Lacking Complementary Dispositions

Misplaced validation sources are the root issue to countless relational dysfunctions. In the rubble of our brokenness we often take our inner questions to sources of approval and comfort other than God. Our drive for approval is an inborn need, but trying to satisfy this need in an invalid manner only leads to chaos in our lives. When we allow our insecurities (housed in the old and fallen nature) to drive our need for affirmation, we fail to live in the wholeness and completeness of Christ.

> Misplaced validation sources are the root issue to countless relational dysfunctions.

This manifests in seeking validation and fulfillment from other things or other people. Relationally, this results in three main symptoms: 1) people playing the image management game, 2) people relating with either competitive or clingy dispositions, and 3) people with addictions, attempting to numb the root issue.

Think about your own relationships. Does your insecurity or low self-worth drive you to hide in a pattern of image management based on what you believe is required for acceptance by others? Does your insecurity lead you to *compete* with others for attention or superiority…or perhaps to seek *to complete*, or *be completed by* another? Or are you numbing the pain of fear-based beliefs about yourself with a substance, a person or a situation; in other words, with an addiction?

Let's examine the patterns of our life to gain clarity. Although it may seem easier to cover up the chaos by sweeping it under the rug, or by believing the lie, "That's just the way I am," we must learn to recognize our own misplaced validation sources.

The Fig Leaf of Image Management

In the attempt to cover internal insecurity, image management is the fig leaf worn by a culture obsessed with external validation and others' opinions. In Western developed nations billions of dollars are spent every year to cultivate an image crafted to impress as many people as possible. This is seen in all the virtual personas of the social media craze. Facebook is the perfect environment to carefully curate one's life in order to seem as impressive as possible. The number of "likes" and reposts by "followers" feed the need for approval and are false measures of one's real value. The age of selfies feed the need for more attention. Brilliant masks are painted based in a mix of the fear-of-rejection and self-importance.

In addition, self is our idol too frequently. But maybe you don't rampantly take and share selfies. Yet are there not other ways we play the image management game in the effort to build up or protect what others may think of us? Over the years, the most disturbing place I've experienced this game is sadly, among church members. Its insidious nature impacted my life greatly.

As a child I was aware of demands, some spoken and some unspoken, to project perfection. I grew up in a legalistic church and knew what was expected, struggling even at a very young age with what I saw as hypocrisy and inauthenticity. It wasn't until I got burned by attempting to defy that culture that I would understand how often it's deeply embedded in the relational patterns of very well-meaning Christians.

I was a young wife and mother attending a ladies' Bible study at a pastor's wife's home, and here I let my guard down. Instead of relating in my normal self-protective manner, I decided not to play the image management game that day, not knowing the sting of rejection was to be my reward. Prayer request time came for the group and I simply followed directions as had been given. We were to write down the heaviest burden of our heart for which we were praying.

I should have just followed the lead of those that had gone before me, but I did not. I exceeded the group's norm and chose to be authentic. Deciding to trust the group and expose a vulnerability, I was honest.

The ladies looked away. Some knowingly glanced at each other. The pastor's wife quickly nodded and graciously indicated she would be praying for me, and then swiftly went on to the next "burden" shared in like-manner as those prior. The following woman's aunt was having bunion surgery. Appropriate murmurs of empathy sounded from around the circle since the group seemed to know the elderly woman mentioned as a member in the church.

But my mind was reeling in confusion, lost in my own thoughts. Really? Wait—what just happened? While dutifully trying to muster empathy for the lady with bunions and her concerned family, I was completely bewildered. I had just shared the heaviest burden of my heart as requested. We were all married to people in ministry. I thought they took the Word to heart. I thought they really understood prayer as the means to intercession. I asked them to pray against the negative spiritual impact my (first) husband's law enforcement career was having on him personally and upon our marriage and children.

So what was with these women? All the talk of family members' surgeries and vague requests for "more grace or wisdom," revealed nothing of depth. They kept everyone at an emotionally and spiritually safe arm's length. How could it be that I was the only one in a group of more than twenty who actually had a real burden impacting relationships at the deepest level? Was I really the only one being targeted by a spiritual enemy that I knew was in hot pursuit of my marriage and family?

Many years later, I know I was not. The church went bankrupt and essentially dissolved. But in that moment of my life, while yearning for authentic, grace-based relationships, the experience seared a lesson deeply into my heart by my enemy. He didn't want me upsetting the dynamic of comfortable captivity and powerless prayer.

That day I learned how to more effectively don the fig leaf of image management. And I discovered that authenticity was dangerous to the established norm. Christian truisms and trite sayings for feel-good conversations were the safest form of expression in church. I would bear years of pain alone due to the chaos of the enemy's tactic on that day and on many others in various churches over the years.

"How are you?" could not be answered authentically. After all, no one "respectable" ever answered, "Well, I feel like I am going to fall apart or go crazy. Just yesterday I discovered more infidelity going on behind my back. But praise the Lord, while I momentarily considered homicide, the Holy Spirit stopped me before I got the gun out of the drawer."

Instead...I was "fine." But as you undoubtedly know, I was not. And in reality, I know now that many around us today in our churches are not fine either. Like me, they yearn for authentic, safe relationships to encourage them in the battle and to build them up in the Truth. But too often the culture dictates participation in some surface-deep charade of "fine," "fun," and "God bless you."

The game of image management is a huge barrier to meaningful and rich relationships between people, *but more seriously, it's a barrier to intimate relationship with God.* Please read the last statement again. When people become accustomed to shrouding their heart behind smoke and mirrors, over time, they become caged—unable to be honest

> The game of image management is a huge barrier to meaningful and rich relationships between people, *but more seriously, it's a barrier to intimate relationship with God.*

even with themselves. The fig leaf of image management is based in a lie from hell that keeps us covering what we perceive as weakness, compensating for a life full of flaws we'd like to hide.

My life, like yours, in reality is a story made up of good times and bad... prudent decisions and foolish ones...obedience and disobedience...clarity and confusion. *It's a story of redemption untold if hidden by a fig leaf.* When we choose to wear the outfit of pretense because of the ongoing fear of what others may negatively think, we limit the good news of Christ. And that should be a sobering thought.

Fear keeps us clinging to faulty thought patterns that drive this relational stronghold. Each Christian's story has a common theme, whether they're free enough to be honestly self-aware of it or not. It is a story of hurt and healing, sin and forgiveness, bondage and redemption. Until you can fully acknowledge your whole story and in humility be enlightened to the redemptive quality of the experiences God has allowed in your life, you will not be free to live in the wholeness of Christ. You'll remain without the validation you crave, your identity and purpose in Him unknown and untapped. The inner chaos will continue.

Triumph cannot emerge from tragedy without Truth. We'll never know the relational possibilities with God and others until we consciously decide to surrender our attempts at managing our own image. Surrender takes you and me out of the way, allowing Christ to showcase His image. Until we refuse to play the games of the same status quo culture, we will fail to reflect the image of Christ. We will be unable to love sacrificially and participate in complementary relationships.

Decide to be one who sees past the brave smiles. Magnify God's glory revealed through your own gaping cracks of human brokenness. Your authenticity will give permission for others around you to begin to do the same.

The Fig Leaf of Competition or Clinginess

Many dysfunctional relationships also involve those who wear the fig leaf of competition or clinginess. This fig leaf is extremely common as I am sure you will recognize.

In a relationship with a competitor, individuals play the "one-up and one-down" game, thus are unable to engage in complementary dynamics. One person asserts himself or herself as dominant and superior by "putting down" someone else. In large and small ways they compete for superiority and attention.

All competitors must carefully manage a fragile false-self they assert as superior while using other people to feed their need for affirmation. Pride, which is the dependence on self, is the ugly root of this dysfunction. We all need to pray for inner enlightenment and truth since pride easily deceives each one of us. Have we operated out of our false-selves for so long that we are closed to authentic truth confronting our fear-based, prideful thinking? Only a contrite heart will lead you to freedom from faulty thought patterns. God lovingly liberates those who desire the truth to burst faulty self-perceptions.

A person with a clingy disposition is on the other end of the spectrum. They're motivated by insecurities and the need for self-validation just like the competitor. But because they're afraid of being alone, they're willing to take any mistreatment and be inappropriately used to fill their own need for belonging. Clingy people can be overt attention seekers or may be more timid and "mousey." These men and women all seek a sense of worth and approval from the relationship to which they cling, rather than from their Creator.

You may have experienced relationships that are inappropriately entangled, without healthy emotional boundaries. Being part of these types of relationships may have led you to believe you are responsible for managing the emotions of others, but you aren't. A parent who attempts to gain self-worth through their child may inadvertently teach the child that they need to become what the parent wants. Keeping the parent happy becomes the driving force, rather than becoming the person God designed.

A parent with unmet validation needs is unable to complement the child. The adult's own emotional needs will unconsciously define the underpinnings of the relationship. Unknowingly, the parent will use their child to meet their own emotional needs. The cycle of dysfunction will continue if grace doesn't intervene to bring inner healing.

An enabler will also prop up or cover up some sort of unhealthy behavior in another. This "helper" stands in the gap and over-performs to compensate for the under-performance of the other. This was one regrettable trap I fell into. Because I'd been indoctrinated in the image management lie, I enabled a great deal of dysfunction in my first marriage. When an under-performer or addict never experiences the totality of natural consequences for their behavior, the motivation for change is circumvented.

Our efforts to compensate for the poor mental health, immaturity, underachievement, irresponsibility, or addiction of another can never lead to real healing. It only perpetuates the chaos stemming from the inability of both parties to complement one another. And it impacts generations.

Whether competitive or clingy, these individuals offer their need for approval to illegitimate sources. To defy the relational chaos and allow God to intervene, we must first recognize our own real need, and then in humility turn away from faulty thought patterns that have impacted the way we relate to others. Only our Creator can validate us in the manner we need, bestowing emotional health and giving us the ability to offer ourselves to authentic connections.

> Only our Creator can validate us in the manner we need.

When the Truth sets you free real change can occur. Only in this freedom are you able to become part of mutually complementary relationships. We must make the intentional decision to discard the fig leaves of pride and self-dependence showcased as relational competitiveness or clinginess. Only then can we rest in our worth in Christ, relating to others with the goal of giving rather than taking.

The following Scriptural truths paraphrased below may help you identify some characteristics of people who are complementing others:

- *A friend loves at all times...* (Proverbs 17:17)

- *Faithful are the wounds of a friend; but the kisses of an enemy are deceitful.* [A real friend will tell you the truth even if it is painful, while someone protecting themselves will lie or say nothing at all.] (Proverbs 27:6)

- *Iron sharpens iron; so does a person sharpen the life of a friend.* [A healthy friend encourages you to be "sharper" and doesn't dull your edge to thwart your full potential.] (Proverbs 27:17)

Although friends who truly care for and sacrificially love us may be rare and precious, we can decide to be that kind of person for others. We are fully alive in Christ's wholeness and holiness when the image of God living within us is revealed. It is in this state that we are able to authentically encourage and inspire others to become all *they* are intended to be.

✍

The Fig Leaf of Addictions

The last fig leaf associated with non-complementary dispositions is one we don when seeking, in our own strength, to numb the pain of untreated wounds and enemy lies. Offering our wounded hearts and core validation needs to anything or anyone but God can lead us to addictive physiological, psychological and spiritual bondage.

Addictions are symptoms of deeper root issues; they are never the diagnostic cause. In the attempt to meet the need for approval and self-worth, many people self-medicate. Drugs, alcohol, pornography, sex, career, self-injury, food, gambling, relationships, exercise, power—they are all examples of things with which we can be addicted. And while most people in Western developed countries don't generally worship idols of the totem pole and effigy type, we must recognize personally that idol worship is rampant in the form of addictions.

Our idol is what we turn to for comfort and protection from the pain of exposure; a comfortable fig leaf put on at a time when an unmet need is exposed. To relieve the longing or stress, people or things are put into a position only God rightfully holds. This addictive idol, a false-god, has the power to medicate the pain of our heart through deceitful and temporary diversion. But only the one true God has the power to heal. Without healing, the affection and appetite for the addiction grows. What began as a mere foothold in our life becomes a stronghold of misdirected worship.

Many people fail to rid themselves of negative addictive behaviors because they don't look to the root issue. Behavior modification therapy and support groups can certainly be helpful in altering dysfunctional coping patterns and offering accountability. But if *inner healing and transformation* fail to take place, lasting change cannot occur.

Acknowledging you have offered your validation need to other people or things is the first step to healing. You must repent of setting up an idol, a substitute for God, in your heart. Renounce its power in your life as you turn away from it by turning to Jesus. In cases of chemical addictions, recognize that professional medical help may be needed for dealing with the physiological changes occurring in the body and brain. There is no shame in seeking medically supervised treatment to address the consequences of what was put into your body.

> If inner healing and transformation fail to take place, lasting change cannot occur.

It's likely that you'll also benefit from professional psychological help as you delve into past traumas leading you to your fear-based beliefs about yourself. Remember, our experiences and thought patterns burn neural pathways in our brains. The chemistry of our thoughts and feelings is a physical issue that may need an expert in talk therapy to help you understand how your brain and emotions got wired a certain way.

Additionally, find a strong spiritual mentor or faith coach to help you learn and grow in the truth of God's Word, so that you can successfully battle the real enemy. This person will be a source of accountability and will complement you on your transformational journey. They'll help you establish new mental, emotional and spiritual pathways for a renewed mind.

Without relational transformation we risk succumbing to strongholds that will limit the quality of our relationship with God and others. To become part of complementary relationships we must decide to relinquish our role in the image management game, refuse to compete with or cling to people, and repent of our unhealthy addictions.

Utilization of Healthy Boundaries—Pillar Three

Healthy boundaries comprise the third pillar with which to build relationships. God is the creator of boundaries, using them first as the framework for creating order. Boundaries provide clarity and dispel chaos. Do you remember how the darkness was divided by the Light in Genesis 1:4? God dispelled confusion by setting boundaries. In the same way, they help us establish order in our own lives to stop the cycle of chaos in relationships.

> *"God is light, and in him is no darkness at all. If we say that we have fellowship with him, and walk in darkness, we lie, and do not the truth."*

God draws a distinct line in the sand by describing His nature in 1 John 1:5-6. He is light and in Him is no darkness at all. The nature of God contains no shades of grey, no gradient within the shadows. God describes the clear contrast. He is light and if we say we have fellowship with him yet walk in darkness, we are liars. There is no vague ambiguity here. His boundaries let us know exactly where we stand with Him and this provides immense security.

Boundaries established by God lead to abundance, not to lack. This applies to the limits imposed in relationships as well. We are to leave some and are to cleave, or stick tightly to others. (Genesis 2:24) But the way to utilize boundaries in

> Boundaries established by God lead to abundance, not to lack.

relationships is frequently misunderstood. Our primary attitudes toward boundaries are developed in childhood unconsciously. They reflect our parents' skill in building relationships with this pillar.

Defying the Chaos of Relationships Lacking Healthy Boundaries

Just like borders between nations, states, municipalities, and between your own yard and your neighbor's, boundaries define who is responsible for what. They determine where ownership begins and ends. Broken concepts about boundaries are evident when people do not "own" themselves and take responsibility for their own behaviors or when people maneuver to "take ownership" of what is rightfully another's.

Recently, I saw this play out in a literal sense. A couple in my neighborhood spend countless hours to enhance and maintain their lawn, but large ugly arcs of dying grass began to appear along the fence line between them and a neighbor. Interestingly, no ugly dead grass was on the neighbor's side of the fence.

When asked about it, the neighbor defensively admitted he had sprayed grass killer on their side of the fence. With no remorse and no answer for the reason, he exclaimed, "I can do what I want because I own the grass a foot and a half beyond the fence line!"

What? You can imagine the confusion, shock and indignation of the couple. There was no legal evidence of a boundary other than the permanent fence that had existed for many years. No survey had been done to establish new property rights. There had been no warning, knowledge of a dispute or rationale given for the neighbor's action. He purposed to overstep the known scope of ownership and destroyed property nurtured and maintained by others. He then became defensive when confronted about the unacceptable nature of his behavior.

And sadly, so it often goes in relationships. Countless toxic interactions occur in unhealthy relationships made up of those with wounded or flawed interpersonal boundary skills. Think of healthy boundaries as a fence with a gate. The owner of the property *inside* the gate is the gatekeeper, opening it to allow good to come in, but keeping it closed to ensure that bad stays out.

People with this broken pillar get gate management mixed up in one way or another. Some have been conditioned to believe they should never speak up to resist someone else's toxicity. These are the people who avoid conflict at any cost so keep the gate open. They don't know how to keep the bad out. Consequently, untruth is readily dumped upon their life. While they've been commissioned to guard their heart,[4] it's clear they don't value themselves enough to do so.

The person who oversteps the boundaries of others and believes it's okay for them to do so also showcases this broken pillar. Taking on the ownership rights of another may be rationalized as being "nice," or "helpful." But when healthy boundaries are not upheld by both people in a relationship, it's the seed bed for an under-performer and over-performer to establish an unstable pattern of relating.

Attitudes About Boundaries Are Forged in Childhood

Our attitudes about boundaries are imprinted in childhood and are demonstrated by how we allow ourselves to be treated and how we treat others. This ties directly to what we saw within our family of origin. Parents who mismanage their own boundaries and infringe upon the boundaries of others replicate this pattern in their children.

When treated like objects "owned" by the parent, children have their boundaries violated in large and small ways. Healthy parents see their children as souls for which they are accountable to God. They view themselves as stewards of God's creation, accountable to God as they guide their children toward Him. A parent's role is to assist their son or daughter in becoming the unique individual intended by God, helping their child to discover their own gifts and talents.

Families with boundary issues aren't able to do this. Perhaps the mother, out of her own insecurity, and likely while playing the game of image management, routinely thinks and speaks for the child when the child is the one being spoken to. She defines the child's likes and dislikes on their behalf, undermining the child's decisional capacity and the confidence to choose for themselves. Maybe the child is constantly rescued, never given the opportunity to learn the consequence of irresponsibility, growing up to believe others are responsible for his happiness and success.

In these ways and countless others the opportunities to teach the child how to manage their God-given power over *their own* attitudes and actions are lost. In the future, they become prone not only to failing to recognize when others violate their boundaries, but also will fail to respect the boundaries of others.

Attitudes About Boundaries Establish How We Manage Power in Relationships

People with weak boundaries have difficulty understanding the source and scope of their God-given dominion. Individuals either give away their power, believing they have none while feeling helpless, used and victimized—or they exceed the scope of their power by attempting to control that for

> People with weak boundaries have difficulty understanding the source and scope of their God-given dominion.

which others are accountable, along with all the associated circumstances.

God's Word as truth provides the corner posts for defining appropriate boundaries, including the scope of personal dominion while living within relationship to others. God told us to leave some relationships and cleave to others, which establishes the changing dynamics of our dominion in various seasons of our lives.

For example, parents have greater influence or control in a young child's life, but eventually the power base for that child's responsibility fully shifts. In the process of maturity we are to become fully aware of our own accountability to God for our own attitudes, thoughts, words and actions, as well as to the impact of the power we wield through each of these means. A child will learn to exercise healthy boundaries and become an emotionally strong adult when parents personally model understanding of their own dominion within relationships.

A Biblical Framework for Personal Boundaries

While many adults didn't experience Godly modeling in their families of origin, we can scripturally reframe our concepts about boundaries to enable complementary relating. It really comes down to understanding two Biblical keys: the scope of *responsibility* and the scope of *accountability*.

Galatians 6:2 and Galatians 6:5 provide insight. In summary, these verses teach each one of us that we each are responsible *to* others (bear one another's burdens) and *for* ourselves (everyone shall bear his own load). Interestingly, these are not contradictory statements as it might first appear.

*"Carry one another's **burdens**, and in this way you will fulfill the law of Christ."*
*"For every man shall bear his own **load**." (NET)*

The key is the differentiation between the Greek words now translated into English as *burden* and *load*. The word *burden is indicating the weight of trouble* in our lives.[5] These are the trials of our faith; the circumstances God allows in our lives to refine and grow us into His image. But the word load is different, its root meaning is referring to the cargo of a ship. A *load is the necessary elements required in the business of doing life.*[6] In other words, it's the load carried by a responsible adult as required to care for himself and family.

The understanding of personal responsibility for the load of daily living is learned in childhood from emotionally mature parents who model it. The mental and emotional connection between cause (action and accomplishment) and effect (the result and reward of satisfaction) is established when the burden of ownership is placed where it Biblically belongs.

Even though we live in a world that may elevate an entitlement attitude or attempt to redirect personal responsibility, the Biblical mandate to bear my own load is evident. The truth according to God's word is that no one *owes* you or me anything. Not a meal. Not a monthly check. And not a cell phone. We were each given the power to rule and govern our own choices, acknowledging God as our provider. We co-author our own lives with God, according to His grace and within the scope of individual opportunity and the personal limitations that He has allowed.

When ideas about boundaries are skewed, the understanding of one's own individual power is perverted, leading to the belief that *someone else is obligated to provide* for my welfare and happiness. "Someone else is *supposed to* rescue me, clean up my mess and make me happy. Someone else is to blame for my life not going the way I want or if I have less than others." But these statements are simply not true.

Healthy interpersonal boundaries establish that we are individually responsible for the weight of our daily living with all of our own associated attitudes and actions, and not *for* those of others. But before settling into the easy chair too deeply, remember this: we are *accountable to* others as we obey the law of Christ.

The Law of Christ: Our Ultimate Accountability for Boundary Management

According to Galatians 6:2, we are *accountable* to fulfill the *law of Christ*, which is accomplished when we help carry the burdens of another's trials of faith. First, let's gain understanding on what the law of Christ is.

God is love (1 John 4:8) and my acceptance of the sacrifice made by God through the manifestation of Jesus Christ pays my debt to the Old Testament law. Jesus fulfilled that law on my behalf. The intent of God's law has always been love. It was His way to teach us we could not meet His standard of holy perfection and then lead us to His solution found in Jesus. Our accountability in the New Testament is to love others as we have been loved unconditionally by God. It is in this love that we are to demonstrate "other focus" and look to the best interest of others.

But this other-focus is not in response to the demands of another who "expects" it, nor due to a perceived debt or duty for being responsible *for* that other person. Our other-focus is rooted in our allegiance and obedience to

Christ as a demonstration of our love *for Him* as our Savior. It is a good work made possible *because* of His grace in my life, not a way to obtain His grace and favor, or that of any other person.

> *"A new commandment I give to you, That you love one another; as I have loved you, that you also love one another. By this all will know that you are my disciples, if you have love one for another."* (John 13:34-35, *NKJV*)

Jesus' law is to love one another. And it is His love which empowers us to love others according to His grace and truth. He gives us insight with the motivation of Christ's love. Through His wisdom, we realize that exceeding our scope of responsibility, or overstepping a boundary, is not in the other person's best interest, and consequently is not love. Becoming a long-term enabler in the person's life who is failing to bear their own load of responsibility doesn't help them become who God desires. It only short-circuits the consequences which diminishes the motivation to change and grow.

Jesus' love exhorts us to carry the weight of our Christian brother's and sister's trials. Burdens of failing health, broken relationships, unanticipated turns of events, loss of jobs, death of loved ones, and many other trials test our faith and draw us to intercede on each other's behalf. We are to carry these burdens to the throne of grace, petitioning the Father for His intervention and a peace that exceeds human understanding. And then *in whatever manner we are led, because of our gratitude to Christ,* we are to lighten the physical load of others during their trial.

Navigating healthy boundaries and motives can be difficult at times. Being gatekeepers of our hearts requires intention. Loving people with the love of Christ includes utilizing healthy boundaries. Recognizing our accountability to take ownership for what is ours allows others to be responsible for what is theirs. This ultimately showcases God's grace and truth in love. And His truth and love are the only forces that will ever defy the chaos of this world.

Mutual Commitment to Authenticity—Pillar Four

The final pillar upon which to build healthy relationships is that of the mutual commitment to authenticity. A person's capacity for authenticity depends on the degree of commitment to the truth, coupled with the willingness to fully apply it personally. Many people claim they desire freedom and clarity. There is much talk in the world about becoming your authentic self. But truth, as taught in John 8:32 and John 8:36, is the only medium whereby growth is facilitated and transformation is experienced. Real freedom is only attained through the truth. And truth is only accessible as it's sought in humble authenticity.

"And you shall know the truth, and the truth shall make you free." (John 8:32)

"If the son [Jesus] *therefore shall make you free, you shall be free indeed."* (John 8:36)

"Jesus said unto him, I am the way, the truth, and the life: no man comes unto the Father, but by me." (John 14:6)

"Set them apart in your truth, your word is truth." (John 17:17, *NET*)

Truth gives us the ability to connect first with God, with ourselves and then with others. It enables you to "get real" instead living in pretense. Truth releases our caged heart to live in authentic humility, in grace and in love. It frees us to step out of the image management game and let go of any unhealthy comparisons.

A love for the truth allows impostors to take off the mask and relinquish the charade. This freedom in truth allows us to see ourselves and others as God sees. It levels the playing field and shows us that *we are all made of the same stuff*. We are all in need of our Savior and His redemptive power in our lives.

To be authentic is to be released from the delusions and the lies of the enemy. He's whispered for too long that we must conceal our real selves and be ashamed of emotional or spiritual nakedness. But unveiling the reality of our lives clothed in the glory of God *liberates us to operate out of the authenticity of our real-self* instead of the deceit of the false-self. By experiencing this freedom found only in Christ, you are released to transcend earthly circumstances and live a

> Unveiling the reality of our lives clothed in the glory of God *liberates us to operate out of the authenticity of our real-self*

whole and holy life standing in His strength and power, magnifying His name.

So with all the benefits of authenticity, why is then that completely authentic relationships are so rare, even among Christians?

Defying the Chaos of Relationships Lacking Mutual Commitment to Authenticity

We live in a largely inauthentic world that feels no shame in redefining reality and calling truth relative. All of the blurred boundaries and lack of authority generates more chaos. Authenticity represents a distinct rejection of this norm, showcasing a completely different outfit than that which the majority wears. Being clothed by God covers the nakedness of our vulnerability and is reminiscent of how He clothed Adam and Eve.

> *"Unto Adam also and to his wife did the LORD God make coats of skins, and clothed them."* (Genesis 3:21)

The way we choose to dress matters. We can pridefully attempt to cover ourselves with fig leaves of self-righteousness and self-effort or we can accept and display the beautiful garments given to us as a gift by God through Jesus, His Son.

> *"I will greatly rejoice in the LORD, my soul shall be joyful in my God; for* **he has clothed me with the garments of salvation, he has covered me with the robe of righteousness,** *as a bridegroom decks himself with ornaments, and as a bride adorns herself with jewels."* (Isaiah 61:10, emphasis mine)

Christians can refuse to joyfully embrace the outfit with which God adorns us. Too often we deny the reality that on a *daily basis we are in desperate need and without any personal righteousness to adorn ourselves.* By default the old threadbare fig leaves of self-effort and pride display our practical agnosticism. In this inauthentic state, we live a damaging illusion that separates us from an authentic and intimate relationship with God, and with others.

> The old threadbare fig leaves of self-effort and pride display our practical agnosticism.

The benefits of authenticity are immeasurable. Our commitment to being real enables our release from delusion and from the lies of the enemy. It's what allows us to stand in the finished work of Christ, clothed only in His righteousness. And to be clothed in Christ's righteousness is a key element in the quest for living and loving authentically. Being clothed with the right attire is vital.

When we attempt to dress ourselves we cannot be relationally authentic and intimate. Do you remember Adam and Eve? After disobeying God, their first response was not to go and tell Him; it was to hide. While in hiding they designed the very first outfit of self-righteousness crafted from the finest of fig leaves. Humility and authentic exposure was not their natural reaction, instead they created a barrier of deceit. Revealing their state of vulnerability came only after God sought them out. And so it is for us as well.

Our personal efforts at covering up only create hindrances to healthy relationship with God and others. Since we all need the saving grace of God to clothe us, we are no better or worse than anyone else. Self-righteous efforts to dress ourselves up only lead to spiritual and emotional isolation. They separate us from the real person we were designed to be and prevent us from being known and known by others.

But it does not have to be this way. We can be part of strong, intimate relationships with God, ourselves and others by committing to utilize the four foundational pillars defined by our Creator. Your relationships can be healthy, based in life rather than death, transparent yet covered by God's glory shining upon you.

Healthy relationships nurturing clarity rather than perpetuating confusion are built intentionally by those who first know intimacy with Christ. Only in deeper relationship with Him are we able to break the cycle of relational chaos in our families, communities and churches.

Exceed the status quo by knowing the power of Christ within you and by being known for the love it produces. It's in this power that you'll be set free to thrive: relating through authentic connections, experiencing vitality, and creating an eternal legacy.

KEYS TO THRIVE

Know and Be Known.

1) How have your relating skills been affected by your use (or lack) of the four pillars of healthy relationships? (Shared Natures, Complementary Dispositions, Healthy Boundaries, Mutual Authenticity)

2) Only whole and emotionally healthy people can enhance others by bringing out their best. Christians are alive spiritually and are whole in Christ, thus they are best suited to have healthy, authentic relationships. Why is it then that Christian relationships often look no different from those who do not profess any faith?

3) Evaluate how you seek to validate yourself, that is, how you seek approval. Is your ultimate source of approval what God thinks and says about you?

4) Evaluate your thought patterns related to interpersonal boundaries. Are you allowing the good in while keeping the bad out of your heart? (Review Proverbs 4:23)

5) Truth to ponder: Genesis 3:7-10; Isaiah 61:10; Revelation 19:6-8; Ephesians 4:22-24

9

AWAKENING DEEPER DESIRE

Is Your Heart Fully Alive?

"The most powerful weapon on earth is the human soul on fire."

Ferdinand Foch

desire — *noun*

    a longing; an appetite; a hunger motivating action to satisfy its object

Desire from deep within our soul is a wonderful but dangerous thing. Our longings can make or break us, can they not? Think about it; cravings from places we often don't understand can determine our level of health physically, emotionally and spiritually. Consequently, exploring the subject of desire can be viewed as exciting, stimulating fibers of our being once deadened to our conscious awareness, but also frightening because it is risky. It might drive a change. And it might make us feel vulnerable. What if you desire something that seems unattainable, something out of reach, like real freedom and a life that thrives? None of us like vulnerability to disappointment and heartache. Consequently, many have simply learned to avoid thinking about inner freedom and meaning, resigning themselves to an anemic existence.

Desire is the fuel to action or motivation. It's the forged steel in the backbone of a human will and the fire within your soul driving its purpose. But what happens when you've come to the point of deciding to avoid the risk of disappointment by disconnecting from deep desire? Does it matter that you find yourself to be mostly apathetic?

The answer is a resounding *yes*. Apathy, we shall see, is evidence that the enemy has taken the fight out of the warrior. Remember the thief? He wants to steal your eternal reward in exchange for worthless perceptions of safety in this life.

Most of us have been apathetic at one time or another. To this day I know when my own internal switch of disconnection is flipped; do you? Mine was solidly wired during many high risk years while in a relationship that lacked emotional safety. It was a God-given coping mechanism to preserve my sanity during times of shock and crisis. But it could have sabotaged all future relationships and my ability to connect from the heart had I not been enlightened to the enemy's trickery and released from those chains.

The liar claims it's safer to not care, telling you to escape to your emotional bunker. But the bondage of apathy is deceitful and destructive...and dreadfully dark and lonely. The truth is that a heart deadened to desire makes a person vulnerable—not impenetrable. Apathetic Christians become defenseless to the wooing of false lovers, or idols. When we decide

> The truth is that a heart deadened to desire makes a person vulnerable—not impenetrable.

to avoid a painful reality we get set up to be unwitting abettors for the enemy's cause. Living only as empty shells of what we were designed to be poses no threat to his evil agenda.

But I want to advocate for a solution to this insidious bondage. I've experienced life inside and outside its cage, and outside is much better. There is an option available that frees your heart from the fear of vulnerability, allowing you to truly thrive, not just survive. The deeper and true desires of your heart can be met, but it requires making a choice. We must choose to live in the power of redemptive love, the power of a passion that heightens our senses and delivers the abundant life Jesus promises. It was only after I reached the end of my rope and sat among the devastation of shattered dreams that my heart was prepared to desire the power of redemptive love above all else.

Desiring the Abundant Life

Finding the abundant life sounds great on paper you may say; but how? Is it some lofty poetic language that Jesus used in John 10:10 to merely inspire us with a positive goal? New Age thinkers claim solutions to finding this life are found in everything from meditation to the power of crystals and spirit guides. But the real solution is centered on timeless truth, not a crafty counterfeit based in spiritual powers of darkness. *Finding true abundance centers on an authentic and intimate relationship with Jesus Christ.*

Yet real intimacy is contingent upon desire, the lack of which, is the root problem. Let me ask you a few questions to help you evaluate the level of desire you have for this thing called abundant life. Do you remember or can you imagine the intensity and elation of falling in love...

to know that someone loved and desired you, reciprocating the way you loved them? You longed to be with them; their words brought you happiness. You craved their presence and wanted to get to know them more. You desired to please them and intentionally found ways to do so as they literally consumed your thoughts.

So is this the way you feel about God?

How do you feel about Jesus and His divine love for you? Do you desire Him in the way He desires you? Perhaps you're just finding out how much He loves you. And maybe your heart is so consumed by distractions you don't think about it much. I also understand the likely first reaction, "Come on; let's not get weird! Who is really 'in love' with Jesus?"

I get it. Those who love Jesus with an intense desire are certainly in the minority. They are exceeding the status quo of mainstream North American Christianity. Many say they love Jesus with their mouth; it's just that their lives prove they love themselves and the world more. To have the abundant life promised in John 10:10 we must become nonconformists to a so-called faith which is stronger in rhetoric than reality.

> To have the abundant life promised in John 10:10 we must become nonconformists to a so-called faith which is stronger in rhetoric than reality.

The secret is in desiring *to fully know* the love of Christ, the power of His resurrection and the fellowship of His suffering.[1] It is only by desiring Christ in His complete fullness *that we are compelled to fearlessly thirst to consummate our love and bear fruit in the abundant life.*

Understanding The Power of Desire

But desire can also be a messy and formidable thing. It's a motivating power that exceeds cognition and reason, a power that can be used for good or for evil. Desiring to love God and be loved by Him, although good, can feel frightening because it carries us into a new dimension beyond merely ourselves and our own control. But in like manner, succumbing to wrong desires can also be a frightening reality if the object of such is evil.

We must come to see that *desire of the human heart is a powerful force shaping the stories of our lives* in the face of changing circumstance. Desires are easily corrupted and fickle, often selfishly motivated because desire resides within our hearts, a place desperately wicked if not changed by God.[2]

We are warned to guard our hearts diligently for good reason. Your heart is the innermost central part of your individuality and is what makes you uniquely you. It is a place housing tender vulnerability, but also contains the potential for strength and courage. With poetic metaphor Proverbs 4:23 instructs that from within the heart come the well-springs of life: vitality bubbling forth from deep places, defining all you desire.

Because your heart is a place of vital importance it's the object of *contest* and *conquest.* There has been a fight going on for it since before the day you and I were born. Our enemy, a shrewd tactical genius, knows the strategic importance in battling for your heart. Satan knows this is the command center on high ground controlling all other fronts of your life. If he rules your heart, he will be master of your desires.

Even though you may have invited Christ to be your Savior, Satan knows how to wreak havoc in the day to day operations of your life. Our life stories are replete with enemy attempts to sabotage the abundant life of peace and joy God intends for us. He accomplishes this with one central strategy: the assault of our heart.

Long ago calculated tactics were initiated in your life as the devil began using other people to inflict deep searing wounds, scarring vulnerable tissue within. He then infected you with lies and began constructing the bars of our heart's prison. Satan understands better than you and I of what we are capable. If we were to allow the power of the Divine nature to fully rule our heart we would be formidable and unstoppable, standing in the victory of Christ.

Are you now beginning to see the big picture more clearly? He may not be able to keep us out of heaven, but he can prevent us from living a life that advances the cause of Christ.

Too frequently in the bondage of apathy, we fail to showcase the power of Christ's love to a lost and hurting world. We end up perpetuating the enemy's cycles of dysfunction. His assault on you and me as the objects of God's love is relentless. He successfully deadens the power of desire by continuing to bombard us. And as a result, he effectively cancels our mission.

> Satan understands who you are in Christ and the power of the redemptive love living within you.

Bondage of Your Heart Is the Devil's Business

*The devil makes it his business to keep Christians in bondage... He knows that it is no use trying to damn a forgiven and justified child of God who is in the Lord's hands. So, **it becomes the devil's business to keep the Christian's spirit imprisoned.***

He knows that the believing and justified Christian has been raised up out of the grave of his sins and trespasses. From that point on, Satan works that much harder to keep us bound and gagged, actually imprisoned in our own grave clothes.

He knows that if we continue in this kind of bondage, we will never be able to claim our rightful spiritual heritage. **He knows also that while we continue bound in this kind of enslavement we are not much better off than when we were spiritually dead.** [A. W. Tozer, emphasis mine][3]

Although alive spiritually, we can choose to live this life in chains, enslaved to the devil. Satan blinds the minds of those who need spiritual birth and uses similar tactics on Christians. The various barriers of bondage prevent the desire for true intimacy with God and yield the ultimate failure in the life of a Christian: no desire, thus no surrender to His consummate love.

Satan dulls our longings and destroys the capacity for intimate delight in the Lord. *God desires for us to long for Him* just as He longs for real relationship with us. His pleasure is to delight you as you delight in Him.

"Delight yourself also in the LORD; and he shall give you the desires of your heart." (Psalm 37:4)

Corrupted Desires of the Heart
Steal God's Promise

Unfortunately, desires are often corrupted or traded for immediate gratification known as human lusts. This happened with the Israelites who were on their journey to the land of promise.

"So they did eat and were well-filled; for he gave them their own desire; they were not estranged [separated] *from their lust..."* (Psalm 78:29-30)

Sometimes God allows us to be filled with our lusts to teach a lesson He knows we can't learn any other way. The Israelites wanted their longings satisfied by something other than that which the Lord had provided. They whined and complained. With a distorted memory of the life they had been saved from, the Israelites set their desires upon a taste from the past. These people, much like us too often, were driven by their own selfishness. They had a perverted perspective of reality, demanding immediate gratification to be "happy."

And so God finally gave them what they wanted.[4] They obtained the object of their lust. But while gorging on all they thought would fulfill them, they suddenly were stopped in their tracks. The children of God came to the sickening recognition that what they wanted was actually a source of death. *Fleshly desires terminated their journey toward the fullness of God's promise, revealing and reinforcing their bondage.*

Lusts of the flesh do the same in our lives as well.

God desires a faithful relationship: one void of perverted affections that compete for His position as Lord of our lives. It grieves Him to see His beloved children in the bondage of disobedience resulting from illegitimate desires. These can never substitute for the sustenance of His love and blessing. It hurts Him to watch us give ourselves away to "false lovers" when we are the love of His life, betrothed and set aside for Him.

"Do not love the world, neither the things that are in the world. If anyone loves the world, the love of the Father is

not in him. For all that is in the world—the lust of the flesh, the lust of the eyes, and the pride of life, is not of the Father, but of the world. And the world is passing away, and the lust of it; but he who does the will of God abides forever." (1 John 2:15, *NKJV,* emphasis mine)

*"And **you shall love** the Lord your God with all your heart, with all your soul, and with all your mind, and with all your strength: this is the first commandment."* (Mark 12:30, *NKJV,* emphasis mine)

God's desire is to have an exclusive love relationship with us, intimate and personal. He wants our heart, and He wants all of it, not just a piece of it.

But this concept presents a problem for most of us. Far too often, we live compartmentalized lives. Getting in touch with your whole heart to love anything could be problematic. Your heart, like mine was, may be fractured and numb in certain spots. Perhaps you've been going through the motions while doing your duty toward God. We would like to thrive in the abundant life, but we have no idea what it might look like and how to attain it. And so we distance ourselves from the idea and survive as I did for years.

The time has now come for you to realize something crucial. If you hope to ever live the life Christ came to give you through His redemptive power, *you must allow your deadened heart to come alive and be roused from apathy.* But to do so, we must first go back and figure out how our hearts ended up in such a state.

> If you hope to ever live the life Christ came to give you through His redemptive power, *you must allow your deadened heart to come alive and be roused from apathy.*

⟳

Recognizing a Spiritual Heart Attack

Whether a severe case of apathy associated with depression or perhaps a more mild case revealed through flippant indifference to things that matter to God, apathy is the principle symptom of a hardened heart. Apathetic people have caged hearts, perhaps unconsciously suppressing emotions like anger, excitement or passion. They lack interest or concern for things others find moving or exciting. Without empathy or compassion they live in a flat world of no color and dimension. Apathy leads to passivity, lethargy, unresponsiveness, insensitivity and lack of commitment. The negative toxicity of apathy is draining to all life around them.

But how does this hardening of the heart happen?

It's a just another result of the invisible war waged against us all. Apathy is the diagnostic indicator of a post combat status I've labeled, PSKDD, *Post Steal Kill and Destroy Disorder*. This spiritual disorder is the result of battle we've discussed earlier. It's the result of trench warfare where the enemy successfully *steals* your faith, *kills* your hope, and *destroys* your capacity to give and receive love. And just like PTSD (Post Traumatic Stress Disorder) it manifests its painful presence in a similar manner: walled off hearts, lack of peace and joy, and loss of potential for a life that thrives.

Seven tactics are used by the enemy in the decent to apathy, which if not deliberately halted in an individual's life will lead to emotional and spiritual bondage. A case of PKSDD renders us unable to love with *all* of our heart as vitality becomes hindered.

These seven tactics equate to seven phases of a spiritual heart attack. And just as you would seek medical attention for the chest pain warning you of a physical heart attack, you must recognize and seek treatment for your spiritual heart attack if you are having one. Your enemy desires to stop your beating heart spiritually, killing your capacity for joy as your heart atrophies in its frozen state.

Phase One: Dissatisfaction - Unmet expectations are dissatisfying. We desire something different from what we got.

Phase Two: Disillusionment - Reality is revealed but our expectations are unmet. Failure to embrace this experience as the doorway to true vision sustains the downward spiral as we entertain dissatisfaction.

Phase Three: Discouragement and Disappointment - If stuck in the place of grieving for lost expectations, an entitlement attitude can flourish as a result of enemy lies. Grief and disappointment must be given to God.

Phase Four: Detachment - The pain of grief and loss overwhelms and we disconnect to cope on our own, effectively distancing ourselves from the discomfort. Walling off ourselves from pain won't resolve the issue.

Phase Five: Diminished Trust - The voice of doubt rehashes your woes and isolates you from others as you take on the role as a victim. We question God's intent and fail to trust Him in our conclusion that life isn't fair.

Phase Six: Diminished Hope - Hope is killed as dejection, despair, and depression oppress the mind with harbored anger. Hope, inextricably linked to our heart's desires, is drained from our outlook on life.

Phase Seven: Deadened Heart (Apathy) - The capacity of your heart's desire to give and receive love (the core of the believer's mission) is destroyed through the deceitfulness of sin.[5] A part of the vital center of who you are has sustained death.

The seriousness of spiritual apathy is clear. We must learn to deal scripturally with our dissatisfactions and disillusionment to prevent their spiraling effects. This life is regrettably full of disappointment. Things don't work out the way we thought they would. At times, people do not follow through on their word and some may betray our trust. Disease sets in and tragedy strikes.

The way we cope with this sin-scarred world will either refine the desires of our heart or deaden them. We'll either become enlightened or incapacitated. The way you respond will lead to a life of clarity and vigor—or confusion and torpor. It is truly up to you.

We each have the opportunity by faith to walk through the door of true vision and victory in Christ. The choice to view our circumstance through spiritual eyes focused on the bigger picture and plan of God requires surrender in the face of uncertainty and sorrow. Surrender keeps our hearts soft as we acknowledge our frailty and need for the shelter of Christ's strength and sufficiency.

Take Heed: Diagnosis and Dangers of a Hardened Apathetic Heart

God provides some clear warnings and instruction to us about this subject of hardened hearts. It's found in Hebrews chapter three. The passage is written to the "holy brothers" who are partakers of the holy calling. Here, both past, present and future followers of Jesus Christ are being put on alert to avoid a hardened heart:

> *"Harden not your hearts, as in the provocation, in the day of temptation in the wilderness."* (Hebrews 3:8)

The children of Israel wandered in the wilderness of sin and grieved God with their repetitive bad choices and calloused state. They provoked His wrath with their apathy toward Him and His ways. We gain insight by studying Psalm seventy-eight as their behaviors and choices are detailed. Regrettably, if we are honest, we must admit we are like them far too often.

Children of God provoke His wrath when:

- They are forgetful of the works and wonders of God
- They fail to set their hope in God
- They don't keep God's commandments
- They are stubborn and rebellious but refuse to repent and correct their course
- They lack commitment and perseverance
- They are driven by lust
- They have their lives consumed by emptiness and chaos
- They flatter and lie
- The limit what God wants to do in their lives
- They refuse to take the high ground He already purchased for them
- They are unfaithful
- They set up idols in their lives
- They induce the delivery of His strength into captivity and His glory into the enemy's hand

We must evaluate our lives every day for the deceit of sin that attacks our heart. Just as occurred with the children of Israel, a foothold of hardness is revealed by behaviors.

Hardened Hearts and Unbelieving Believers

I'll bet you can see some similarities between yourself and the children of Israel just like I do in myself. Why do children of God like you and me harden our hearts? Why would we want to limit God and live in bondage to apathy? Simply stated, it's a pain response.

A hardened heart occurs as a result of the effort to survive a trauma of one type or another. We've all been given an amazing capacity by God to survive. The ability to temporarily dissociate from pain is actually a God-given mechanism. But when taken too far or for too long it produces a hard, dead heart. Whether used to cope with the trauma of abuse, endure the agony a broken relationship or any other disappointment, we must ensure that we don't inadvertently harbor a sinful response to the pain.

The dissociative reaction necessary to survive extreme psychological pain and physical hardship, such as that of the infantrymen during violent, life-threatening combat is not a sin. But if unaddressed, the unacknowledged emotions from the traumatic experience will lead to long-term negative effects. *That which may facilitate survival in the short-term, does not enable life in the long-term.* A hardened heart is not free to thrive because a part of it is walled off and dead. The hopeful heart is one alive. But if hope bleeds out and desire dies from behind a wall, you will find yourself feeling lifeless deep inside…apathetic.

The children of Israel were just "trying to survive" a life in which God had actually purposed for them to thrive.

But they erred in a critical strategy leading to years of wandering, and years of struggle and emptiness. *Their error was failure to know the way of God and to desire Him above all else.* And this is the same error of heart made by many Christians today.

God wants us to thrive despite the circumstances. He delights in orchestrating the desires of our heart when our primary delight is in Him. We don't live fully in the potential that is ours because our hardened hearts don't have the capacity to deeply desire. And God's viewpoint on hardened hearts, apathetic to His way, is clearly stated. In Hebrews He calls them *evil. Evil hearts of unbelief.*

> We don't live fully in the potential that is ours because our hardened hearts don't have the capacity to deeply desire.

> *"Take heed, brothers least there be in any of you an evil heart of unbelief, in departing from the living God.* (Hebrews 3:12)

The paradox of unbelief residing in the heart of a believer is a disturbing inconsistency to ponder. We, as believers in the supernatural power of Jesus Christ to save us from our sins, can still, and often do have issues with unbelief. And this unbelief is a major problem since God calls it *evil.* Evil puts a barrier between us and God. What we fail to believe in, we fail to hope in. And when we do not have our hope in God, we do not desire Him.

Our lack of desire for God puts a wall between that which God desires for us, and that for which we settle. Read that again. We end up living lives of practical agnosticism, weary and worn; surviving, but not thriving. We find ourselves empty because we do not crave the fullness of God. Our desires have become tainted by sin.

"But exhort one another daily, while it is called today; lest any of you be hardened through the deceitfulness of sin." (Hebrews 3:13)

The preventative measure to be taken against a hardened heart is clear. *We need exhortation against sin.* We need this from brothers and sisters who have the compassion and confidence to do so. You and I must be encouraged to avoid the path that departs from the living God. This path is made up of slippery steps leading us to the same place Adam and Eve found themselves after their encounter with the liar.

The consequence of apathy is practical faithlessness. It's a life of futile wandering, just like in the example of the lives of the children of Israel. They had been redeemed from their bondage yet failed to fully trust God in order to enter into a place of confident peace. This is the supernatural peace founded on His divine promises, a place known as the rest of God.

"Now with whom was he [God] angry forty years?
Was it not with those who sinned, whose corpses fell in the wilderness?
And to whom did he swear **that they would not enter into his rest,** *but to them who* **did not obey?** *So we see that* **they could not enter in because of unbelief.***"*
(Hebrews 3:17-19, *NKJV*, emphasis mine)

Let this sink in deeply. Unbelieving believers are disobedient believers. *These believers miss out on the abundant life they were intended to experience because of hardened hearts and lack of desire.*

> Believers miss out on the abundant life they were intended to experience because of hardened hearts and lack of desire.

The Rest of Rest

Jesus personally teaches on the subject of the rest of God in Matthew 11:28-29.

> *"Come unto me, all you who labor and are heavy laden, and **I will give you rest**. Take my yoke upon you, and learn of me; for I am meek and lowly in heart: and **you shall find rest** unto your souls."* (emphasis mine)

He understands the heartache and heavy burden of this life and offers a different way than that based in the futile labor of self-effort. His way is based in surrender.

Matthew teaches us that by coming to Jesus there is first a rest which *Jesus gives*. This rest is given and is based solely in *His action*. The *rest of redemption* is received when we surrender the self-efforts of working our way to God for salvation.

After receiving Jesus' gift, we have the opportunity to find another kind of rest, one we *find* for our souls. This rest is contingent upon *our action*. The *rest of obedience is only found when we surrender* to taking His yoke upon us and learning of Him. It is only through our labor of love, or our obedience, that we find peace and rest for our souls. Far too many Christians have chaos in their lives for one reason alone: disobedience.

> *"Let us labor therefore to enter into that rest, lest any man fall after the same example of unbelief* [disobedience]." (Hebrews 4:11)

You and I must surrender our self-protective, self-advancing and self-righteous ways and trade them for Christ's yoke of humility. Complete dependence on God is the only means to finding the confident place of resting. *Dependence is the path to desiring God and the abundant life. It leads to falling in love with Him, the lover of our souls.* In surrender to become *one with God* your heart will become free to rest in His embrace. You will be *in* love—because God *is love.*

False-Lovers Deaden Our True Desire

Too often however, believers settle for a pseudo-relationship with impostors who deaden our desire for intimate relationship with God. Our involvement with these false-lovers causes us to feel disconnected from any need for intimacy. Just as a woman prostituted and abused will psychologically detach when repetitively used as an object to fulfill the selfish lusts of others, we detach when used by our enemy for his evil purposes.

We discussed in the last chapter that anything or anyone taking the place reserved in your heart for God is a false god, an idol. They package themselves in different ways for different people, but false lovers promise immediate, yet illegitimate, gratification to some legitimate need. They divert our attention from a spiritual hunger for the power of Christ by assuaging our superficial craving for satisfaction. Whether a traditionally labeled addiction to alcohol, drugs, sex or food, or the more subtle idols that could be your child, career, or money, they all accomplish the same thing.

Idols medicate instead of heal. They all are saboteurs posing as saviors. Any false lover is a barrier to intimacy with God because He demands total commitment and monogamy of heart. But we may not be self-aware enough to discern God's spirit as He attempts to show us that we have false

> Idols medicate instead of heal. They all are saboteurs posing as saviors.

lovers freeloading within. We become desensitized to what *should* be because of how it's *always been*.

A Christian may stay stuck, unable to grow and find deeper intimacy with Christ because of footholds established during complex histories that include unhealed wounds and unbroken agreements with the enemy. Kyle Idleman does a masterful job in his book, *gods at war,* showing Christians how idols affect each of us. I recommend it for a more detailed exploration of this subject.

In Joshua 24:14-15 we are given an example to follow regarding getting rid of life-controlling idols. In the process of maturity and growth (known as sanctification in the Christian's journey) we see God bringing His children, the Israelites, to a place of distinct choice about the type of relationship they will have with God. They were given the choice to serve God in sincerity and in truth, thereby experiencing the promises of God fulfilled in their lives. Or they had the option to serve the false gods they'd picked up along the way and face the withdrawal of God's blessing while enduring His chastening during a life of futility.

Their leader, Joshua, exhorts the people to evaluate the three ways idols may have become a part of their life, declaring they must choose between the true God and the false gods. You and I must also apply this exhortation. Evaluate how idols may have gained a foothold into your "normal" way of thinking, feeling and coping without you realizing it.

The text first details the *gods of our fathers or ancestors.* These idols were *erected in our family of origin.* Consider what you were taught by the pattern lifestyle of your parents. For what did they sacrifice and adore (i.e. worship)? Self, career, image, material things, productivity, efficiency, etc...? How much of what you now choose is related to your parent's method of coping or validation? Do you hear "ghostwriter" voices (like a parent) affecting your choices in the way you live your story? Are they defining what you "should" or shouldn't do to manage your stress or be accepted?

Scripture then lists the gods of our fathers *back in Egypt.* These idols were picked up while living in the *world's culture and value system prior to the exodus of redemption* (sex, money, entertainment, exterior beauty, etc...) Consider how your priorities and pursuits are affected by a God-defying world-view. Are your decisions about what consumes your time and what brings you comfort grounded in a Biblical world-view as opposed to the value system of the world?

Last are the *gods of the Amorites, in whose land you are living.* These idols are those *in close proximity.* They take us unaware, hidden in plain sight. Consider how you make everyday seemingly mundane decisions. For example, evaluate the food you eat and why, the clothes you choose to wear and why, the way you spend your private time and steward your money, etc...

Dare to Desire: Be Awakened to True Love

To be awakened to an authentic, unconditional, and captivating love, we must quit clinging to any pet idols we've allowed in our lives. We inflict deep grief on our Savior and Bridegroom when we choose to sleep with the enemy. He paid the ultimate price to redeem us from the prison manned by our enemy's arsenal of false gods.

> To be awakened to an authentic, unconditional, and captivating love, we must quit clinging to any pet idols we've allowed in our lives.

The first step in allowing yourselves to be awakened to true love is to admit that you haven't protected yourselves from idols as warned to do in 1 John 5:21.

"Little children, keep yourself from idols."

But getting rid of an idol is more than an intellectual exercise of will-power or the emotional response of sorrow; it involves breaking old spiritual covenants with the enemy. Only then can old desires be replaced with the desire for an abiding relationship with your True Love.

First and foremost, it involves repentance of the heart. You must intentionally turn away from the idol and call your involvement what it is: sin. I had to repent of everything from the idol of self-reliance through my career to stress-management through a sugar addiction.

Second, it requires opening up your yearnings to respond to God as the source of love already given. God is love and it is this love of God that compels our deepest desire to love Him because He first loved us. My prayer now is that I can love Him in the way He desires to be loved as I stand in awe of His unfathomable, unwavering love for us.

We all were created with the desire to thrive. But for far too many it's a longing that's been dormant, shrouded by apathy and held captive to false lovers. Thriving fully in who you were created to be is to live the abundant life. Becoming awakened to God living through us stirs our zeal for giving and receiving real love. Our awareness in each moment of His presence and power is peaked as we learn to live in loving response to His prompting for intimate connection.

And so it is time to choose for yourself.

What is your heart's desire?

Will you choose the power of redemptive love and be released from the bondage of a hardened heart?

Are you ready to remove any barrier preventing you from passionately loving God with all of your heart?

I pray that we, like Joshua, will choose to renounce the power of false gods. We must intentionally open ourselves up to the fullest blessing, accepting the power of God's love as it penetrates deeper, choosing to live for a greater cause than self.

"As for me and my house, we will serve the LORD."
(Joshua 24:15)

Exceed beyond the norm...dare to desire real love... the redemptive love of God.

KEYS TO THRIVE

Dare to Desire.

1) Has your heart ever been deadened by apathy—and is it now?

2) Do you see in your own life how your heart, the core of your being, has been strategically the object of contest and conquest?

3) What does the following quote mean to you personally?

   "*The devil knows if he can keep the Christian bound and gagged, actually imprisoned in our own grave clothes we are not much better off than when we were spiritually dead.*" (Tozer)

   Are you bound and gagged?

4) Think about the differences between a true desire of the heart and lusts of the flesh. Which are you allowing to write your story?

5) Truth to ponder: Psalm 78; Psalm 37:4; Galatians 5:16; 1 John 2:16

10

BECOMING REAL

Are You Ready for a New Dimension?

"You become. It takes a long time.
That's why it doesn't happen often to people who break easily,
or have sharp edges, or who have to be carefully kept.
Generally, by the time you are Real, most of your hair has been
loved off, and your eyes drop out and you get loose
in the joints and very shabby.
But these things don't matter at all, because once you are Real you
can't be ugly, except to people who don't understand."

Margery Williams, *The Velveteen Rabbit*

The ache to come fully alive and thrive, to become all you were designed to be, is a yearning placed by God within each of our hearts. Unfortunately, most people never reach their full potential. Instead, their life story reflects the status quo illusion, the product of passive choice, the failure to live with any particular end in mind. Being set free to thrive, as we've discussed throughout this book, is clearly not a result of passivity. Those stuck in a victim's mentality believe the lie that "life happens to them." These swallow another blue pill while remaining plugged into ignorance and inaction, trapped by fear-based thought patterns of blame, excuses and denial. With no vision into the larger reality of what is and is to come, they do the best they can to survive.

Regrettably, Christians also find themselves living as victims rather than victors. With no personal demand for change, or any call for deep thinking, many are easily conformed to the captivity of mediocrity. But as we have been learning, the opportunity to live a transformed life in an enlightened reality persistently calls to the hidden places of our heart. God awakens our desire for more.

But just as experiencing life requires getting out of bed and not merely opening our eyes while passively lying there, so does a victorious life lived in the power of redemptive transformation. Intentional participation is required, but this is where we can get confused.

The power of victory is not in trying harder.

The action required on our part: *surrender.*

Surrendering to live humbly and authentically in the power of God's grace and redemptive plan is the key to the abundant life. Only then can we transcend, or rise above all circumstances to experience the abundance of peace and joy that He alone can deliver. In surrender we finally get real, fulfill our mission to glorify Him, and in

> Surrendering to live humbly and authentically in the power of God's grace and redemptive plan is the key to the abundant life.

the process become transformed. This is the key for living in the new dimension of full reality and for knowing our place within it.

But is authenticity and connection to the power of God in a meaningful way really possible? And if so, is it sustainable? For years I too, wondered.

While begging for grace through the storms of martial betrayals of the worst sort, I plead for God's insight and wisdom. I knew the biblical grounds for ending the relationship were present but didn't have peace to do so. Through Casting Crown's 2003 song, *Stained Glass Masquerade,* the God's Spirit asked, *"Is the love of Jesus enough to make you stay?"* My answer was yes. And by His strength and grace I would transcend the circumstances of another cycle of sorrow.

But the plastic people were all around me. Their masks were garishly smiling and uninviting as I processed the pain of my trials alone yet again. I played along in the same game of pretense to maintain the status quo, keeping others who preferred surface level relationships comfortable. But I yearned for a place to be real, a place where I could come out from the protective walls that defended the painful wounded places of my heart. Instead, I donned my own smiling mask and murmured clichéd replies to trite questions while wrestling with God. Little did I know that He was using the chaos to completely undo me to bring me to a place of total surrender and inner healing.

Yes, Lord. Yes, You are enough to make me stay. You're enough to mold me and make me into the woman you desire me to be. You are enough to give me the strength to live as your trophy of grace while in deep sorrows of a private hell.

By the time my dreams completely unraveled and I found myself unwillingly single, I desired even more of His redemptive power. I'd been released from a dark pit and was closer to greater vision and healing, but I was still in bondage, unable to see clearly. There was more calling me. I desired to be transformed, to see and experience the power of divine reality in the midst of a broken life—and that was exactly God's desire all along.

In my search, I discovered an amazing woman named Mary. Her name means, "bitterness or sorrow," a life theme I understood far too well. Her story will add meaning to your life as it did to mine.

Someone We Understand

Mary's world had once been filled with bitter chaos that sought to overwhelm and define her, to confine and limit her. She was a woman with a questionable background. Countless unfounded speculations about her morality have been proposed throughout history. She could have easily played the victim. Mary was acquainted with the broken life…a life scar-pocked and ruined by untold stories of abuse, emotional and spiritual agony, loneliness and sorrow. Adding to her heavy burden, was the cool snobbery and judgment of others who scorned that which they did not understand.

You see, she was well-acquainted with affliction, a captive in a prison beyond her capacity to control. Her life was unmanageable. The power of the enemy had imprisoned her, weaving dark threads through the tapestry of a life destined for more. The complexity of who she was as a person remained unknown by those whose own fears and insecurities led them to oversimplify, quickly label, and then distance themselves from the full reality of the opportunity for an unfolding miracle.

In some regard I wish I could say that I cannot relate to all of it, but the truth is, I can. Those black threads are in my tapestry, and in each person's I've met who is willing to be honest. These are the threads woven in by someone else's decisions, some else's words, someone else's selfish values…someone else's sin. And in addition, we each have those threads representing desperate moments of our own…our stumbling and falling, our lunging for control instead of falling back on faith. I see my dark threads and remember when the enemy's agenda seemed to be positioned for victory…where black cords like tentacles of evil wrapped tightly around my heart. I soberly remember circumstances used in the attempt to destroy the beauty and life-giving force issuing from the deep reservoirs of divine promise within me.

Oh yes, I can relate to Mary, the afflicted one.

But then, as often occurs in great stories, everything unexpectedly changed. Mary was miraculously delivered. The power of God's grace intervened. The bars of imprisonment were broken and shackles fell away. She was lifted from that dark pit of isolation and loneliness, and praise be to God, so was I. She was changed through a personal encounter with Jesus. And that life change was much more than an emotional experience for her; *it ignited a powerful process fueled by the power of redemptive transformation.*

Her desires were awakened. And *she desired Jesus in the full reality of who He is.*

Mary's deliverance liberated her, making way for the miracle of a transformed life. Living fully alive as never before, she unveiled the beauty of who she was in Christ, and executed her mission. She would accomplish all for which she had been created, fulfilling all God predetermined in the story *He* wanted written *through* her. And that's what I want. I long to satisfy all God desires to write through me. Do you?

> She would accomplish all for which she had been created, fulfilling all God predetermined in the story *He* wanted written *through* her.

A compelling three-part framework for knowing this transformational power is given to us through what we know about the life of Mary. Intentionally applying it will bring us the reality of renewed vitality through Christ's redeeming work within us. We must recognize our captivity, desire deliverance and surrender for the climax.

Recognize Captivity

To know transformational power in our lives we must first consider that *our captivity may be tied to that which distinguishes us* from others with whom we share many similarities. This particular woman named Mary was set apart from other women named Mary by the attached reference to her home town, Magdala. In Jesus' day it was a thriving coastal town on the Sea of Galilee approximately three miles from Capernaum, known for its textile industry, linen dying processes, and its unsavory culture of harlotry.[1]

Mary Magdalene is how she is identified. She was a follower of Jesus, who in the face of whatever the known facts were about her, was labeled by her earthly city of origin. Some have taken great liberty to surmise she was one of the town's harlots. But the Bible tells us nothing about her age, lineage, upbringing, or occupation. We can surmise that she was a woman of some financial means because of her ability to minister to Jesus and the apostles after her conversion, but the Bible doesn't give us these details. Perhaps she was a widow or a spinster. Maybe she was an entrepreneur; we simply do not know. And in the end, it really does not matter. God gave us what He wants us to know about her, and what we do know has the power to change us, as it did her.

The name of Mary's home town, Magdala, in Greek means, "tower." This is of some interest for you and me to consider from a spiritual applicability standpoint. A tower in a coastal town during the days of Mary served as part of a defensive system, erected to keep watch against invasion and subsequent harm to the inhabitants. It was a means of early recognition and communication to initiate fortification against threats looking to capitalize on vulnerabilities at locations of potential insecurity.

We humans have towers of defense as well, would you agree? Regrettably they came as part of the package from the fall back in the Garden of Eden. We tend to use them because they are readily available and familiar, but human-based defense mechanisms are deceitfully ineffective against our real foes.

Like us, with personal defense mechanisms entwining her nature, Mary had to take the first step toward freedom by becoming real with herself, God and others. She had to recognize the captivity originating in the facade of her own towering nature and then in humility turn to God alone for refuge.

"My defense is of God, Who saves the upright in heart." (Psalm 7:10, *NKJV*)

"The name of the LORD is a strong tower: The righteous run into it and are safe. (Proverbs 18:10, *NKJV*)

Jesus knows you by name, but how are you known and identified by others? What towers of defense distinguish you, but keep you in bondage? Intentionally turning solely to Christ for your defense is the first step toward the transformational, healing power we desire.

Desire Deliverance

The second necessary component of the framework for our enhanced reality is to desire deliverance from barriers to deeper intimacy with Christ. It's not enough to just recognize captivity; we must also from the heart, desire liberty. A Christian cannot experience deliverance from the inner bondage of their fear, shame, mediocrity, and unhealthy habits until intentionally stepping outside the prison doors. They've been opened by Christ's victory on the cross over the power of sin and death, but far too often we stay in our old cells.

This is an important and missing concept for some and worth reiterating. While we were immediately released from the *penalty* of sin when we asked Jesus Christ to be our Savior and Lord, it is a daily process to be delivered from the *power* of sin within us. The power of sin is that which seeks to bind us, afflicting us even after becoming Christians. This power of sin, in its many forms, is that from which we need delivered on a daily basis.

Mary is known by her story of deliverance, the story of her life-changing transformation. She is known as Mary Magdalene, *healed of seven demonic spirits*. It's a title of powerfully understated simplicity. The intimate story isn't detailed in scripture for us. But we know Jesus freed her from complete spiritual captivity. She was delivered from the power of darkness and her life changed in form and function. Mary was wholly converted; she was transformed.

Perhaps Mary had been known as a public spectacle, the host of seven demonic spirits with evil intent causing her to do things she would not have done otherwise. She was "that woman," at times likely behaving as a lunatic, words spouting and limbs flailing. Probably unkempt and disheveled, her eyes like pools reflecting the inner torment, dead and cold. Whatever the scene may have been, we know that her reasoning capacity, the power of positive thinking, or any other human based resource couldn't create a changed life for Mary. She was defenseless against the predator of her soul.

*"Jesus expelled from her seven devils who had held her nature as a gang of pirates might seize a man and employ a vessel which they had torn from its legitimate use."*² Mary's life was redeemed one day by Jesus. We can only imagine the relief, peace and joy flooding her soul as the Savior commanded her captors to depart.

Each of us as Christians must apply her story to our own. Christ expelled Satan from our lives when we asked Him to be our Lord and Savior. Think about it. What is your personal story of deliverance? For starters, fill in your name as you read the scriptures below:

"[The Father] has delivered us [**state your name**] *from the power of darkness, and has translated us* [**state your name**] *into the kingdom of his dear Son."* (Colossians 1:13)

"But you [**state your name**] *are a chosen generation, a royal priesthood, a holy nation, His own special people; that you* [**state your name**] *should proclaim the praises of Him who has called you* [**state your name**] *out of darkness into His marvelous light."* (1 Peter 2:9, *NKJV*)

As Christians, we each have a story of deliveranc, *but are we known by it,* as was Mary? Is the story regularly brought to our mind, fanning the flame of our desire for the One who rescued us from the bondage of spiritual death and captivity? Do we remember that we were imprisoned by an enemy, unstoppable through any human tower of defense? What title is given to you by our Lord who knows your back story?

After salvation the memory of our hopeless fallen state apart from Christ deepens our love and thirst for Him day by day. It's the "before" leading into our "after," that when remembered, deepens our gratitude and desire to love Him as He desires to be loved.

Mary's story had power, as do ours, because of her before and after. She didn't try to keep it a secret, but lived an unrestrained life as she embraced her story fully. The enemy seeks

> It's the "before" leading into our "after," that when remembered, deepens our gratitude and desire to love Him as He desires to be loved.

to silence us with tactics of fear and misguided validation sources to short-circuit the victory we have in Christ. We are afraid of rejection and far too often, even at church. Rather than boldly acknowledging the full reality of our deliverance stories and allowing God's healing power to permeate our being and encourage others, we feel embarrassed and inadequate. Fearing the black threads becoming evident, we keep the beauty of the tapestry hidden, tightly folded within ourselves. While this may protect us from the mouths of gossips and the judgment of self-righteous, modern-day Pharisees, in our fear, we end up settling for far less than God had for us.

We live without power.

This described my world for much of my adult life. I trusted Jesus to deliver me from my sins and tried to live in a Christian manner. But the power of His redemptive love wasn't experienced until I let go of all my trying…to measure up…to be accepted…to be loved. God wanted me desperate for Him. It was only after I was delivered from the lies that began binding me in the story of my *before*, that I could embrace the tale as it's woven into God's larger epic of the *after*.

I had conformed to a culture that was full of people doing the best they could, all trying harder, smiling, ministering and serving, *yet unconnected to a deeper dimension of reality in intimacy with Christ.* Since that time I've discovered many were also hurting deep down and felt alone, just like me. It seems clear to me now that we must do something different to get different results in our lives and in our churches.

If you want to live in the power of a transformed and transcendent reality like Mary did, you must defy the status quo, sometimes even at church. Your personal conversion from darkness to light is a story in which we see the awe and feel the gratitude. Your story is your miraculous representation of the redemptive power of God's grace, and it's only in this power that you can make the impact and leave the legacy you yearn for.

> *Your story is your miraculous representation of the redemptive power of God's grace, and it's only in this power that you can make the impact and leave the legacy you yearn for.*

Mary's story, just like ours, is ultimately told to *showcase the Deliverer.* And perhaps this is why God does not give us the details of Mary's afflicted past. Far too many times, I've heard Christians telling stories of their past life experiences or trials that end up, perhaps inadvertently, glorifying the drama of all they'd endured. They become distinguished victims, pulling the heart strings of the audience and garnering deserved but distracting sympathies, but not magnifying Christ and solely glorifying Him.

The main character of our story must never be overshadowed by the understudy. *The presence of Jesus on stage must not be usurped by the narrator.* If this occurs, the transforming power of the story is lost in the blur of rousing, feel-good, tear-jerking moments of the moment. Please internalize this important truth: *Our past story is not what defines us, it merely sets us up for the climax: the rescue, the redemption, and the transformation. Our deliverance is never merely about us.*

While we each are beloved and pursued by Christ, He does so for His glory, not ours. He is the hero, not us. Deliverance from the power of darkness to the kingdom of light is most importantly *about the story the delivered is now equipped to tell about the Deliverer.* Read that again. The delivered (you and I as Christians) have been given an ongoing story for one purpose only, and that purpose is to magnify the Deliverer, Jesus Christ.

> Deliverance from the power of darkness to the kingdom of light is most importantly *about the story the delivered is now equipped to tell about the Deliverer.*

My story is not about me. It is about Jesus and what He has done in me and through me by His power and might, not because of any strength I can claim as my own. Mary understood this. The power of her deliverance transformed her life. The story of her past connected her to the present and shaped her future *because she chose a real and intimate relationship with her Savior and Lord.* He promised her a future and a hope, a reality that exceeds this world.

We too are Christ's trophies of grace. *It's in the reality of our powerful stories of deliverance that the work of Jesus Christ is magnified. The hearts of others can be reached with His love as we authentically connect on the common ground of human brokenness, entirely without hope prior to meeting Jesus.*

And so the issue comes back to what we've discussed before: our desire for the power of redemptive love must be awakened if we are to become all we are intended to be. We must recognize our need, then desire deliverance from fear and shame to fully live in that power. Refusing to forfeit the full reality purposed for our life stories as Christians, we must intentionally come out of the shadows of the old prison cell. We must embrace the reality of our full story and let the power of love change us for our good and His glory.

Surrender for the Climax

The last component to the three-part framework for becoming real in the power of Christ's redeeming work is surrender. It's not striving, or working harder, but to give ourselves up. This surrender to obedience is the labor to enter into His rest, as discussed in a previous chapter. In Luke 8:1-3 we read that Mary Magdalene followed Jesus and the twelve disciples as He went "preaching and showing the glad tidings of the kingdom of God." (Luke 8:1) We learn additionally that she, along with other named women who had been "healed from the afflictions of evil spirits and infirmities, *ministered unto Jesus out of their substance*." (Luke 8:2-3)

These women demonstrated their devotion to Christ for rescuing them from the power of the enemy, *not by acting out of a sense of duty, but out of passionate desire*. They wanted His cause to advance and were willing to give all they possessed for His mission. We are told these grateful followers gave to Jesus out of their *substance*, a word of powerful meaning.

Think about it with me, the substance of something is the actual matter of a thing as opposed to the *appearance* or shadow of a thing. Its substance is its *reality*. Mary and the other women had substance; they were authentic, real, and weren't living for mere surface appearances. They lived for the cause of Christ out of the depths of their substance. *They declared with their lives the reality of the power that delivered and transformed them.*

These women weren't motivated by a desire to *appear* a certain way. They weren't driven by a need to be validated by others, nor by a desire to bring attention to themselves for giving money, time or other resources. They were no longer motivated by the opinions of others, they simply worked to advance a mission: the glad tidings of the kingdom of God.

They knew the strength for advancing this mission wasn't in trying harder; it was the *complete surrender* to something…or more correctly, *to someone* completely beyond themselves. Their desire to minister to Jesus defined their purpose. It was a desire that sprang from deep within their being, poured out *in grateful sacrifice to advance the cause of their Deliverer.*

As redeemed believers in Christ, we too possess substance, but far too many stay lost in the emptiness of a charade while doing their duty. Some are duped, told as I was early in my Christian life that a good Christian is the one who tries harder to be like Jesus. And while I understand what well-meaning people may have been attempting to communicate, this messaging clouds the truth.

The truth is, trying harder is not surrender. Trying harder in our own power leads to frustration, failure and shame. Trying harder means relying on will-power and behavior modification. It can look like change, at least temporarily on the outside, but a changed exterior doesn't transform the inside. And this is exactly why we continue to be bound by the power of our old sin nature.

> The truth is, trying harder is not surrender.

The enemy shames us into believing we are not trying hard enough, calling us failures when we inevitably fall. Shame then leads to hiding, and so the posing and pretending continue both inside and outside the church. We wish we could be real, but don't know what else to do; too afraid of rejection, most play it safe and remain part of the captive norm.

So here is the *"soul-ution"* simply stated: *the solution for your soul is to give up.*

Admit that you can't be like Jesus by trying harder. Empty hands raised high, surrender and die to your own strength and power.

There will be no climax of surrender until we relax solely in Christ's sufficiency, none of our own. Because of Mary's surrender, she was the first human to experience the ultimate climactic experience of relationship with the risen Christ. Ponder this: she was graced with the privilege of being *the first human to see the power of the resurrection with her own eyes!*

> *"Now when Jesus rose early the first day of the week he appeared first to Mary Magdalene, out of whom he had cast seven demons."* (Mark 16:9, *NKJV*)

What? Jesus did not reveal Himself first to one of the twelve disciples? Not to John or Peter? Not to His earthly mother? Not to the religious leaders? No, Jesus revealed the power of His resurrection first to this gratefully surrendered woman. One whose life was delivered from sorrow and bitterness; rescued from an enemy whose power she could not withstand.

Jesus showed Himself first to a person whose past was publicly flawed, but who *knew beyond a doubt the reason for which she had been delivered.* He revealed Himself first to one who was known by, and who knew her story of deliverance. The manifestation of His redemptive, resurrection power was to one whose heart was bursting with love and longing for her Savior. One who had ministered to Him out of surrendered authenticity, not the striving of appearances or duty.

> *"Jesus said unto her, Touch me not; for I am not yet ascended to my Father; but go to my brothers, and say unto them, I ascend unto my Father, and your Father; and to my God, and your God."* (Jesus to Mary Magdalene at the tomb - John 20:17)

Greater Intimacy Through the Power of the Resurrection

This interaction between Jesus and Mary, revealing the power of His resurrection, was the beginning of greater depths of intimacy in their relationship. When we finally see the power of surrender in our own lives as real and not mere rhetoric, we too will enter into deeper intimacy with Christ. The power of death had been eternally defeated and Mary was the first to know it in this physical dimension. What a climax to the story: her name was the first human name spoken by the mouth of the resurrected Son of God. With a heart overflowing with joy, she wanted to cling to him, to hug him to her—but he stopped her.

> *"She must never know Him again in the flesh, but enter into a spiritual relationship which would give her deeper draughts of throne water from higher up the stream, satisfying divine capacity with the divine."* [3]

The privilege and honor of knowing the resurrection power of Christ was not to merely relieve her from the emotional burden of her human grief. It marked a new chapter, *a new way of interacting with God for all of eternity.* And it wasn't only for her, but for all of mankind.

A new way to commune with the Divine had been made and she was not given this revelation to keep for herself. *She was to share the news of the life-altering work that had been accomplished.* Jesus had risen, breaking the power of death and hell, and He was ascending to not only His Father and God, but to *our* Father and God.

Jesus had a bigger vision that included moving Mary to *a place of deeper insight spiritually* as He commissioned her to share her experience with others. And this is the vision He has for you and me today as well.

She was chosen to be a divine witness of the divine capacity for divine beauty within: *the real beauty of the divine nature, Christ in us, the hope of glory.*[4] Surrendered to shine with the allure of His nature internally rather than striving to emulate Him in the power of the human flesh, she began to understand the teaching He'd given about the Vine. He had taught that as a branch is to the vine, she had to be one with Him, to abide in the True Vine. Her joy would be made full as she was filled with the fullness of God.[5]

> Her joy would be made full as she was filled with the fullness of God.

Abiding in Christ, which means to know Him in intimate oneness, is the linchpin to the *abundant life: a life based in the divine dimension of reality.* Our divine capacity can only be filled by surrendering all aspects of our being to Him.

"He must increase, but I must decrease." (John 3:30)

I must know Him and the power of the resurrection must consume me. His redemptive love will change us if we *know it intimately* and in complete authenticity.

"That I may know Him, and the power of His resurrection, and the fellowship of His sufferings, being made conformable unto His death." (Philippians 3:10)

"To know the love of Christ, which passes knowledge, that you may be filled with all the fullness of God." (Ephesians 3:19, *NKJV*)

The fullness of God will not be experienced without desiring more than a casual or intellectual knowledge of the love of Christ. We must thirst for the fullness of Jesus' divine nature, who is the Alpha and Omega, the Almighty God, our Creator, our Savior, our Lord.

> The fullness of God will not be experienced without desiring more than a casual or intellectual knowledge of the love of Christ.

"I am Alpha and Omega, the beginning and the ending, says the Lord which is, and which was, and which is to come, the Almighty." (Revelation 1:8)

"And he said unto me, It is done. I am Alpha and Omega, the beginning and the end. I will give unto him that is athirst of the fountain of the water of life freely." (Revelation 21:6)

The reality of our wholeness and holiness is found only in the nature of the Divine living through us. We cannot partake of that divine nature unless we are drinking from the fountainhead of throne water, the eternal, transcendent and life-giving flow. And we cannot drink, unless we first thirst for something greater...something substantive...something deeper...something higher.

So I ask you: *for what do you thirst?*

You and I must exceed the norm of this shallow, chaotic life and thirst for something above ourselves and beyond this superficial dimension. Our life stories become fulfilled when we desire transformation and embrace a new and divine dimension of reality, found in the power of the resurrection.

Our life stories become fulfilled when we desire transformation and embrace a new and divine dimension of reality, found in the power of the resurrection.

"But whoever drinks of the water that I shall give him will never thirst. But the water that I shall give him will become in him a fountain of water springing up into everlasting life." (John 4:14)

We must choose to embrace what we're designed to become in our redeemed identity and divine purpose. We are nonconformists in this world, not bound by its deceit. *We are set free to thrive, living extraordinary lives for the glory of Christ, pointing the way to freedom for others.*

As the reality of our life story continues to be woven into His, we are continually transformed to exceed in this world of chaos.

Fully alive and finally free, you'll become increasingly authentic in a deeper dimension—in the power of God's redemptive love. This is the power that delivers us from the chains of fear and confusion, liberating us for a life of vitality.

Abundantly real...living in real abundance...for the present moment in our once-upon-a-time story...and forever.

KEYS TO THRIVE

Exceed in Life.

1) Write out your personal story of deliverance to include where Jesus found you, how He drew you to Himself and what your life looks like today *because of Him.*

2) Think about how the following statement impacts your life, "Trying harder is not surrender." Is there anything you need to surrender to the greater power of Jesus Christ, rather than continuing to try harder in your own power?

3) The power of the resurrection, revealed first to Mary Magdalene, was due to a relationship built on authenticity and devotion to Christ's mission. This devotion to His mission initiated greater depths of divine capacity from an abundantly divine source. Are you living in the power of the resurrection?

4) Is Philippians 3:10 your personal prayer?

5) Truth to ponder: John 4:14; Revelation 21:6; John 10:10

NOTES

CHAPTER 1: ONCE UPON A TIME AND NOW

1   *The Holy Bible, King James Version*, Deuteronomy 32:4, "He is the Rock, his work is perfect..."

2   *The Holy Bible, King James Version*, Genesis 1:26, "And God said, Let us make man in our image, after our likeness: and let them have dominion...over all the earth."

3   *The Holy Bible, King James Version*, John 8:12, Jesus speaking, "I am the light of the world: he that follows me shall not walk in darkness, but shall have the light." See also, *The Holy Bible, New King James Version*, Colossians 1:12-14, "And giving joyful thanks to the Father, who has qualified you to share in the inheritance of his holy people in the kingdom of light. For he has rescued us from the dominion of darkness and brought us into the kingdom of the Son he loves, in whom we have redemption, the forgiveness of sins."

4   *The Holy Bible, New International Version*, 1 John 4:8-9, "God is love. This is how God showed his love among

us: He sent his one and only Son into the world, that we might live through him."

CHAPTER 2: THE FOG OF WAR

1   Eugenia C. Kiesling, "On War Without the Fog", *Military Review*, 2001 and Joint Service Command and Staff College Course notes, 2001, *Wikipedia*, accessed 11/15/15, https://en.wikipedia.org/wiki/Fog_of_war.

2   James H. Strong, *Strong's Exhaustive Concordance*, Baker Book House, 1991, John 10:10, Greek no. 622, apollymi.

CHAPTER 3: LET THERE BE LIGHT

1   See John 1:1-14.

2   See John 3:19-21.

CHAPTER 4: PERSPECTIVE IS EVERYTHING

1   *The Godfather Part II,* 1974, Mario Puzo & Francis Ford Coppola.

2   James H. Strong, *Strong's Exhaustive Concordance*, Baker Book House, 1991, Proverbs 7:5, *zuwr*, Hebrew no. 2114.

3   Ken Page, "Psychology Today," *Power of the Gifts We Hide: Our True and Our False Self,* December 17, 2013, https://www.psychologytoday.com/blog/finding-love/201312/the-power-the-gifts-we-hide, accessed January 15, 2016.

CHAPTER 5: THE POWER OF SIN'S BITE

[1] "The Philosophers Mail, Teaching Emotional Intelligence" *The Great Psychoanalysts 1: Donald Winnicott*, http://the-philosophersmail.com/perspective/the-great-psychoana-lysts-donald-winnicott/, accessed January 15, 2016.

[2] See Luke 4:5-6.

[3] See 2 Timothy 2:26, 2 Corinthians 10:4, 2 Corinthians 2:11.

[4] See Colossians 2:9-10, Hebrews 10:14.

[5] See Hebrews 10:30, Romans 14:11.

CHAPTER 6: BEHOLDING YOUR IDENTITY

[1] James H. Strong, *Strong's Exhaustive Concordance*, Baker Book House, 1991, *chayil*, Hebrew no. 2428.

[2] See Proverbs 1:7, Proverbs 9:10, Proverbs 8:13.

[3] James H. Strong, *Strong's Exhaustive Concordance*, Baker Book House, 1991, *idou*, Greek no. 2400 and *eido*, Greek no. 1492.

[4] See Ezekiel 28:17.

CHAPTER 7: I MUST BE ABOUT SOMETHING

[1] Viktor E. Frankl, *Man's Search For Meaning*, Beacon Press, Boston, 1959, 2006, p. 76.

[2] Viktor E. Frankl, *Man's Search For Meaning*, Beacon Press, Boston, 1959, 2006, p. 72.

3   See 2 Corinthians 3:6 and 5:18-19.

4   See 2 Corinthians 4:10-11.

5   See 2 Corinthians 3:11-15.

CHAPTER 8: DEFYING RELATIONAL CHAOS

1   Timothy Keller, *The Meaning of Marriage: Facing the Complexities of Commitment With the Wisdom of God, New York,* Penguin Publishing Group, 2011, p. 101.

2   James H. Strong, *Strong's Exhaustive Concordance,* Hebrew no. 813, *ataktos.*

3   Richard Barrett, "Evolutionary Coaching: An Introduction to the Ego-Soul Dynamics of Personal Growth" (Presentation, World Business and Executive Coach Summit, June 6, 2016).

4   See Proverbs 4:23.

5   James H. Strong, *Strong's Exhaustive Concordance,* Grand Rapids, MI, Baker Book House, 1991, *baros,* Greek no. 922.

6   Ibid, *phortion,* Greek no.5413, Grand Rapids, MI, Baker Book House, 1991.

CHAPTER 9: AWAKENING DEEPER DESIRE

1   See Philippians 3:10.

2   *The Holy Bible, King James Version* , Jeremiah 17:9.

3   A.W. Tozer, *I Talk Back to the Devil: The Fighting Fervor of the Victorious Christian,* Camp Hill, Pennsylvania, Wing Spread Publishers, 1972, 1990, 2008, p.3.

4   *The Holy Bible: King James Version,* Numbers 11:4-34.

5   *The Holy Bible, King James Version,* Hebrews 3:13 (hardened hearts) 1 John 4:8, John 13:35 (love).

CHAPTER 10: BECOMING REAL

1   Herbert Lockyer, *All the Women of the Bible,* 1967, Zondervan, Grand Rapids. MI.

2   Dr. FB Meyer, *Biblical Character Sketches*, 1896, James Nisbet & Co., London.

3   Ibid.

4   Colossians 1:27 - "To whom God would make known what is the riches of the glory of this mystery among the Gentiles; which is Christ in you, the hope of glory."

5   See John 15:1-11.

ABOUT THE AUTHOR

Kaye Carter's passion and purpose is to connect people with substance for their soul so they can live with inner vitality. As an author, speaker and life coach, she helps free individuals and groups from the bondage of faulty thought patterns so they can create lives that thrive.

After years as a successful nurse and healthcare leader, Kaye struggled with her own awakening to greater purpose. Realizing her core motivation was the languishing condition of the human heart, she left her corporate position behind to embrace her mission to advance the health of souls. As founder of Exceeding Life, she now serves to inspire and equip those who desire renewed vision, vitality and victory.

In her free time, Kaye enjoys reading, travel and the beauty of the outdoors. She and her husband, Greg, are blessed to live in the Midwest near their four children and five spunky granddaughters.

Connect at KayeMCarter.com for additional resources, to book a seminar or speaking engagement, or for coaching services.

Made in the USA
Charleston, SC
31 December 2016